Loving God With All Your Mind

Equipping the Community of Faith for Theological Thinking

Thomas R. Hawkins

DISCIPLESHIP RESOURCES

PO BOX 340003, NASHVILLE TN, 37203-0003
www.discipleshipresources.org

Cover and book design by Nanci H. Lamar

Edited by Linda R. Whited and David Whitworth

ISBN 0-88177-398-0

Library of Congress Control Number: 2004104682

DR398

Contents

CHAPTER ONE

Keeping in Touch With Teaching

Why Think Critically and Creatively About Christian Faith?

As disciples of Jesus Christ, we are constantly weaving the frayed threads of our lives into vibrant patterns of meaning and hope. We seek to live rich, authentic lives in the midst of often puzzling and sometimes disturbing circumstances. Amid a global family torn by terror and violence, we cultivate Christian communities that can be a sign, instrument, and foretaste of God's coming reign.

Living lives that become the gospel is not easy, however. We wonder whether our choices are consistent with gospel values. We ponder and analyze events as we struggle to be faithful to our baptisms. We join a long line of God's people who have sought to make sense of Christian faith. After the shepherds departed, Luke tells us, "Mary treasured all these words and pondered them in her heart" (Luke 2:19).

Pondering the meaning of our experiences is not always a comfortable task. It sometimes brings us face-to-face with hidden assumptions, flawed understandings, and incomplete knowledge. Mary's ponderings led her to Anna and Simeon, who spoke of a wisdom that would pierce her own heart and reveal "the inner thoughts of many" (Luke 2:35). Integral to Christian teaching and learning is the capacity to think critically and creatively about our personal and communal experiences so that we can make sense of Christian faith.

KEEPING IN TOUCH WITH OUR EXPERIENCE

Four congregations scattered across North America face puzzling dilemmas that demand creative, faithful responses. Listen to their voices:

"The Church Council appointed us to explore alternatives to the current Sunday morning schedule," May Rondolfo explained to her newly formed task force at Trinity Church. "The current schedule creates multiple conflicts. If the children's choir rehearses before the service, then children are not in Sunday school, which causes the teachers to feel upstaged. If children stay in Sunday school, then they do not rehearse before singing at the 10:30 service, which leaves the choir director and worship committee upset. When the church council adopted our current schedule last fall, their solution did not address the fundamental issues. In fact," May concluded, "it only produced more problems. Our task is to balance all these needs in a new Sunday-morning schedule."

Some members shrugged their shoulders. Others looked tense and anxious. None felt the task force could possibly find a solution that met everyone's needs. Scanning the room, May felt her task was doomed from the beginning. How could she help the group think outside the box?

Sunday school teachers at St. James Church found themselves venting their frustrations at the education-committee meeting. "Half the kids in my fifth-grade class are on medication for attention deficit disorder, hyperactivity, or some mood disorder," said one teacher. "Their parents make sure they take their medicine Monday through Friday; but they don't worry about it on weekends. These kids show up on Sunday just climbing the walls. A lot of discipline problems would disappear if we insisted that parents keep their kids medicated all weekend." Another teacher chimed in: "When I first started teaching, kids could sit quietly and listen to you read for the whole Sunday school hour. Now they can't sit in their chairs for three seconds."

Pastor Carlos Woodward's head was still spinning as he sat down at his desk. A state inspector had unexpectedly visited First Church's daycare program and found multiple code violations. The inspector had threatened to close the program unless the church corrected all violations within two weeks. Carlos could already imagine the angry phone calls from parents.

Even if the board of trustees could find a contractor to make the necessary repairs on such short notice, where would the church find money to pay for them? What could the church say to busy, overstressed parents who depended on the church's daycare? The daycare director had left red-faced, flustered, and angry. She had been too upset to think about a solution. "How can I help people stay cool enough to solve this?" Carlos wondered.

Sonya Barnes looked aimlessly out her kitchen window. It was Tuesday. Tonight was her adult Bible study on Mark's gospel. She found herself vaguely dreading tonight's session rather than eagerly anticipating it. The class seemed dull and flat. There was no juice, no energy. Participants gave tired, routine answers. They did not seem challenged or provoked to deeper reflection. "I've got to find another way to teach," Sonya mused. "I'm not getting the results I want. But how?"

New Challenges Demand New Ways of Thinking

In her book *Keeping in Touch* (Discipleship Resources, 1999), Carol Krau proposes that changing circumstances and God's call require us to develop a new framework for Christian teaching and learning. Cultural, demographic, and technological changes have rendered many of our traditional approaches outdated. Krau proposes that Christian educators respond to these kaleidoscopic changes by keeping in touch with five themes: God, God's people, experience, the world, and teaching itself. Keeping in touch with these themes enables Christian educators to discover new patterns for teaching and faith formation in a changing world.

Learning to Think About How We Think. The earlier examples highlight the significance of Krau's proposal. May Rondolfo and Carlos Woodward both confront complex problems with no easy solutions. Today's congregations exist in turbulent environments where the unexpected happens with increasing frequency. Forces outside the congregation and even beyond the local community impact churches in surprising ways. First Church's daycare program finds itself caught in a complex web of state and federal regulations. In addition to these legal and economic forces, unpredictable and ever-changing social circumstances—including changing family structures, consumerism, and volunteerism—influence how Carlos Woodward and First Church respond.

May Rondolfo finds herself caught in the crosscurrents of conflict and dissatisfaction as she redesigns Trinity Church's Sunday schedule. Everything is connected to everything else. Previous solutions have created new problems rather than produced a lasting resolution. She must address a challenge that does not present itself in a neat package. She faces a highly complex, problematic, and contingent "mess"—not a neatly defined problem that yields to easy analysis and intervention.

May and Carlos face unanticipated challenges with ill-defined dimensions. Many groups and people are involved. Actions taken to alleviate stress on one constituency will heighten pressure on another. The situations will grow increasingly complex and unpredictable as events unfold.

May and Carlos respond to situations that are costly in both time and money. They are working in emotionally charged environments where rational problem solving is difficult. Neither find easily identified precedents for what they must do. They instead forge their own solutions in the present situation's messiness and confusion.

Few church educators or leaders experience only challenges that are easily anticipated, predictable, and well-structured. Nor do they encounter problems for which they have readily available solutions based on past experience. Christian educators instead confront situations that are unexpected and novel, messy and ill-structured. These situations are difficult to predict, and they are costly. Addressing them requires outside-the-box thinking. It demands thinking that is critical and creative as well as faithful to Christian faith and practice.

Many Christian educators search for "add-water-and-stir" solutions to these dilemmas. Plenty of authors and consultants peddle "how-to" manuals to satisfy this demand.

In the past, such approaches often worked. Life changed slowly. People and churches were relatively similar despite geographic or demographic differences. Cause-and-effect relationships were easily understood in stable environments. Once someone developed a workable solution, it could be applied to other instances of the same, recurring problem. Results could be formulated into ten principles or seven steps that others could duplicate.

But our world is no longer stable. Nor is it characterized by slow change and simple cause–effect relationships. We instead move at the speed of change. Erratic, unpredictable changes buffet individuals and churches. New technologies leapfrog over older ones. Equipment and solutions that work today are obsolete tomorrow. Instability, cultural differences, and rapid technological change produce unpredictable, messy, and ill-structured situations. A tangled mess seldom yields to an "add-water-and-stir" solution.

Church leaders and educators consequently find themselves disappointed when they follow someone else's recipe. The cake never tastes quite right because the ingredients, the kitchen, and the oven are never the same. More important, the cooks are never the same. Church educators must instead discover how to think creatively and critically about their own experience and context, about the nature of teaching and learning, and about the Christian faith. Only their own reflective, critical, creative thinking can empower them to respond faithfully to the messy, ill-structured challenges confronting them in classrooms and committees.

The solution, Krau proposes, lies in keeping in touch with teaching. In a world where everything feels increasingly complex and problematic, church educators can no longer simply recall and apply previous knowledge. New occasions teach new duties. Today's educators need the capacity to "think about how they think." They need the ability to understand their assumptions and thought processes. Keeping in touch with teaching provides precisely such a perspective. Keeping in touch with teaching helps church educators think about how they are thinking. Recent research in teaching and the brain provides teachers and leaders with important clues for responding to the ill-defined, unexpected, and complex challenges they encounter in classrooms and committees.

Learning How the Mind Processes Information and Learns

Sonya and St. James Church's teachers face a different challenge. Sonya intuitively understands that learning is about change and growth; but she does not see the fruit of transformation in learners' lives. She longs to see deeper personal change and greater spiritual transformation in her students. But she lacks tools and strategies for transformative learning.

Sonya's previous classroom experience has taught her that learning involves the acquisition of new information. So she carefully prepares handouts, lectures, and discussions. She communicates as much information about the Bible as possible. Yet much recent research on the brain and learning suggests that critical reflection, not information, plays a pivotal role in transformative learning.

When Krau proposes that teachers keep in touch with teaching, she is inviting Sonya to reflect critically on new developments in brain research and its growing implications for teaching and learning. Keeping in touch with teaching could make Sonya's classroom come alive. It could change her students' lives.

St. James's Sunday school teachers are also aware that they are not fully connecting with their students. While Sonya blames herself, these teachers are blaming their students. They complain that students "just aren't the same." They observe an increase in the number of children taking medications that alter brain chemistry and functioning. These medications are the fruit of research into how the brain works. Healthcare professionals have incorporated these new insights into their practice of medicine. But educators—especially Christian educators—have been slower to appreciate neuroscience's implications for teaching and learning.

St. James's teachers reflect a traditional attitude that children are "blank slates" onto which teachers etch information and knowledge. The teacher's role is to convey new knowledge primarily through textbooks and workbooks. Imitative behavior, not deep learning, is the goal. Traditional religious catechisms work in precisely this way. A series of questions—usually based on the Apostle's Creed, the Ten Commandments, and the Lord's Prayer—are asked in a fixed order with set answers. Students memorize the correct answers in the proper sequence. While many congregations might be horrified to teach from such a fixed catechism, the underlying pattern of how they teach may not be much different.

Recent brain research reveals that learning occurs in a much richer and more panoramic fashion. Learning takes place when multiple connections are made simultaneously between ideas and experiences. Keeping in touch with teaching would help the teachers of St. James Church discover that teaching is a creative, interactive process that begins by meeting people where they are—even if where they are is bouncing off the walls. Meeting people where they are involves understanding the characteristics of cognitive development and how these characteristics are rooted in the physical development of the growing brain.

Conclusion

This resource will delve more deeply into what Krau describes as keeping in touch with teaching. It will explore the discoveries of neuroscience—the new science of the brain—and look at their implications for teaching and learning.

God created every organ in our bodies for a purpose. The heart pumps blood. The lungs transfer oxygen. The brain learns. The brain learns because that is what God created it to do. That is its purpose. The human brain has an almost inexhaustible capacity to learn. It detects and recalls patterns. It remembers. It can learn from experience and self-correct. It has the capacity to create something novel and new.

We sometimes struggle in our teaching and learning because we have not fully grasped the richness of what the human brain can do. Keeping in touch with teaching means discovering how the human brain changes, processes information, and learns. These discoveries have immediate and profound implications for Christian educators and leaders.

This resource will discuss Jean Piaget's theory of cognitive development. Piaget's work has immediate implications for teachers, particularly those who teach children and youth. Chapter 5 will also look at two theorists who build on Piaget's understanding of how the mind develops and changes: Lawrence Kohlberg and James Fowler. Both have important things to say about teaching and learning for faith.

Interspersed with these probes into the new science of the brain and its cognitive theorists will be practical teaching strategies that emerge from this research. These strategies guide educators in creating settings that cultivate more faithful and transformative learning.

Sonya will find renewed enthusiasm for her Bible study when she possesses not only a broader understanding of how participants learn but also specific tools that allow her to foster genuine, deep learning. St. James's Sunday school teachers will move beyond blaming students and their parents as they acquire both new theoretical insights and practical tools for creating a climate of Christian learning and growth.

May Rondolfo and Carlos Woodward both desperately seek ways to think creatively and critically about the challenges confronting them. They can approach these challenges more confidently when they understand the richness of the human mind and possess methods for critical, creative, and faithful thinking.

This resource is for May and Carlos, for Sonya and the Sunday school teachers at St. James Church. It is for Christian congregations who hunger for a deeper transformation and a more authentic faith. It is for educators who yearn to equip Christians to love, know, and serve the God made known in Jesus Christ.

Deepening Your Learning

> *Each chapter of this book will conclude with exercises or questions that encourage you to deepen your learning. While you can benefit greatly from reading this resource alone, a powerful way to enhance the quality of your learning is to read and discuss it with others. Working through this resource with a group of colleagues or friends is, in fact, consistent with what we will be saying about Christian teaching and learning. As a group you can talk about and reflect upon your perceptions and perspectives. You can together explore the exercises that deepen learning.*
>
> *As you start this journey, who are some people you can invite to join you? A small group of six to eight people is ideal for a weekly discussion of these chapters. You will need to decide who will facilitate each session. Will one person assume this role, or will the responsibility rotate among members of the group?*
>
> *As a group, you will function more effectively if you adopt some ground rules for your meetings. Ground rules will be briefly described in Chapter 6.*

As we begin, you might reflect on:

1. What do you hope to learn from reading this book? What is your hunger? Your yearning? How do you hope to be different than you are now when you finish this book?

2. Who have been your most memorable teachers? What did they do to have that impact on you? In what ways do they influence how you now teach or lead?

3. What does it mean for you to think about your thinking? How often do you pause to reflect not on what you are thinking but on how you are thinking about it? How can thinking about how you think change who you are as a Christian educator and the way you teach?

4. Consider your thinking by completing the following statement:
   Right now, I believe my thinking as a Christian educator is of _____ _____ quality. I base this conclusion on _____ _____.

In these areas, I think about how I am thinking:

1. _____

2. _____

3. _____

In these areas, my thinking is OK but I could do better:

1. _____

2. _____

3. _____

In these areas, I can improve my thinking:

1. _____

2. _____

3. _____

CHAPTER TWO

Fearfully and Wonderfully Made

What We Are Learning About the Human Brain

Keeping in touch with teaching involves discovering what educators and researchers are learning about the human brain. Recent decades have brought significant advances in understanding how the brain processes information, learns, and remembers. These discoveries have important implications for Christian teaching and faith formation.

The human brain is small enough to fit into the palm of the hand yet large enough to contain the whole cosmos. As Robert Sylwester points out, it is responsible for *Hamlet* and the holocaust, for apple pie and atrocities beyond comprehension, and it has created the Sistine Chapel and the silicon chip.[1] It dreams things that have never been and asks "why not?" And it conjures up nightmares that disturb our sleep. All this creativity and terror are held in three pounds of tissue containing nerve cells that number in the tens of billions. Just thinking about the brain is a mind-boggling thought! The human brain is quite literally a cathedral of complexity.

FEARFULLY AND WONDERFULLY MADE

Pondering the miracle of life, the ancient psalmist marveled at God's providence in creating the human body.

> For it was you who formed my inward parts;
>   you knit me together in my mother's womb.
> I praise you, for I am fearfully and wonderfully made.
>   Wonderful are your works;
> that I know very well.
>   My frame was not hidden from you,

when I was being made in secret,
  intricately woven in the depths of the earth.
Your eyes beheld my unformed substance.
In your book were written
  all the days that were formed for me,
  when none of them as yet existed.
How weighty to me are your thoughts, O God!
  How vast is the sum of them!

Psalm 139:13-17

These words describe the complexity and wonder of the human brain. Intricately woven, the brain is both fearfully and wonderfully made.

While we can hold what some have called a "three-pound universe" in the palm of our hands, it is quite large relative to our total body weight. A 150-pound man or woman has a brain weighing three pounds. By comparison, a sperm whale weighs several tons but has only a seventeen-pound brain. The human brain also consumes a huge percentage of the body's energy. It is around two percent of the body's weight but devours twenty percent of the body's energy. Eight gallons of blood flow through it every hour, supplying it with oxygen and nutrients. Along with all this blood, the brain requires a steady supply of water. Dehydration can manifest itself as lethargy and reduced learning. Making sure children in particular have plenty to drink is an easy and important step teachers or parents can take to improve learning.[2]

The human brain has the consistency of a soft avocado. It can be cut with a dull butter knife. Yet billions of cells are packed within it. A mouse has about five million neurons. A monkey has ten billion. But humans have one hundred billion neurons.[3] There are more neurons inside a brain than there are trees on the entire planet. And the number of connections between these neurons might be greater than the number of all the leaves on all these trees.[4]

In addition to neurons, we have another one thousand billion glia. These cells are amazingly small and highly interconnected. Approximately thirty thousand neurons or three hundred thousand glial cells would fit on the head of a pin.[5] Each neuron has separate sending and receiving extensions that are continuously communicating. As a result, the human brain has a virtually infinite capacity for making connections.

The brain continuously uses these connections to process information. It digests experience the way the stomach digests food. It is always responding to the complex world in which it is immersed. The brain's interconnectivity predisposes it to search for connections and patterns. It has an innate drive to make meaning. This drive to create meaning from the buzzing, blooming confusion of life makes learning possible. Our brains learn because that is what God designed them to do. The brain has a virtually inexhaustible capacity for learning.

Other organs like the kidneys or the liver seem to have stopped changing after their form matched their bodily function. The brain, on the other hand, continued to change. Different parts of the brain reflect different stages in our history as a species. We share some parts with reptiles or mammals. Others are distinctively human. All are highly interconnected. Information flows between them in multiple directions. While each part is distinct, no part functions independently, but all the parts work interdependently as a single system.

To imagine how the brain's subsystems interrelate, poke your index finger through the hole of a bagel and then balance a sheet of paper atop of it [see Figure 2.1].

Figure 2.1: A Model of the Human Brain

You now have a rough approximation of the brain's three major subsystems.

1) Your extended index finger represents the oldest portion of the human brain: the brainstem and cerebellum. The brainstem controls many of our automatic functions like breathing and blood circulation, and the cerebellum maintains the body's balance and muscle coordination.

2) The bagel wrapped around your index finger depicts how the limbic system is wrapped around the brainstem. The limbic system is the second part of the brain. It developed atop the brainstem and is fully realized only in mammals. The limbic system is composed of several small structures that communicate chemically with every cell in the body. It is responsible for feelings of playfulness, nurture, shock, and fear. Without a limbic system, we could not bond emotionally with others or create lasting relationships. The absence of a fully developed limbic system in reptiles explains why lizards and snakes do not form close emotional ties but dogs, horses, and humans bond with others.

3) Finally, we have a sheet of paper draped over our bagel. Draped atop our limbic system and brainstem is the newest part of the brain: the cerebrum and neocortex. Sometimes called the cortex, this part of the brain distinguishes human beings from frogs and horses. The human cortex is like no other. Its large size relative to the whole brain and the amazing amount of specialization it displays are unmatched in the rest of the animal kingdom. Thought and speech, deciding and planning reside here.

The brainstem, limbic system, and cortex form three interconnected subsystems that make up the human brain: our triune brain [see Figure 2.2].

Figure 2.2: The Triune Brain

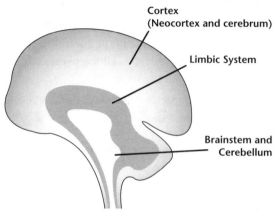

Cortex
(Neocortex and cerebrum)

Limbic System

Brainstem and
Cerebellum

Each part of our triune brain thus has a different history. These differences have important implications for Christian teaching and faith formation [see Figure 2.3].

Figure 2.3: The Triune Brain and Human Behavior

Brainstem and Cerebellum	Limbic System	Cerebrum/Neocortex
Survival Instincts	Feelings and Emotions	Rational Thought
Automatic Processes	Play and Bonding	Choice and Will
Inflexible Routines	Warm Relationships	Conscious Planning
Reactions Without Thinking	Thinking With the Heart	Higher-Order Thinking
Cold-Blooded Actions	Warm Connections	Enlightened Reasoning

THE BRAINSTEM

Together the brainstem and cerebellum make up the oldest and most primitive portion of the brain. Although the cerebellum represents only one tenth of the brain's volume, one half of all the brain's neurons are found there.[6] The brainstem-cerebellum complex regulates our basic bodily functions, cycles, and defenses. We share this brain function with reptiles and other lower species.

Understanding Our R-Brain. The brainstem and cerebellum can be described as our reptilian or R-brain. It regulates involuntary processes such as circulation and respiration. It acts without thinking to preserve life. We cannot stop breathing, even when we try. Nor can we consciously alter our heartbeat. Our bodily cycles and rhythms are automatic. Precisely because they are automatic, they cannot be creative. In many instances, this is a good thing. Who wants the heart to experiment with a different rhythm? Would we want the ear and eye to exchange functions just to see what happens?

The R-brain's goal is survival. It acts without thinking to fend off perceived threats and dangers. Our fight instinct resides in the R-brain. A few nights ago, I was driving home and suddenly a deer leapt in front of my headlights. Before my eyes had fully registered a blur of brown fur, my foot was on the brake. I did not have to think about this process. It was involuntary and automatic. Sensing danger, my reptilian brain acted to defend itself against a potential threat. Most of the time, I am grateful for these automatic responses. They protect me from unsuspected dangers and sudden threats.

On the other hand, the R-brain's lack of originality makes it a slave to precedent and habit. The R-brain does not think in terms of choices and options. It does not weigh alternatives. It adheres strictly to inflexible routines, rituals, and precedent. Such behaviors work against adaptation to change. Consequently many reptiles have only a narrow range of conditions in which they can survive. Beyond these ranges, they perish because they cannot adapt. We too resist new ideas and changes when we downshift into our R-brains. People and organizations perish when they let their R-brains do all their thinking.

The R-brain's obsession with survival can also result in a cold-blooded reptilian determination to survive at any cost—even if it means suffering and loss for others. The R-brain is thus responsible for much of human aggression. It is also responsible for the deceptive behaviors we share in common with reptiles. Lower animals deceive in order to forestall a predator's attack. The chameleon blends into surrounding colors. The lizard freezes in its tracks, not moving a muscle. These R-brain behaviors can take the form of lying, pretending, or faking among humans.

Downshifting Into Our R-Brain. Under certain conditions, the R-brain wreaks havoc on our thinking and learning. This phenomenon is called downshifting.[7] Our R-brain immediately takes charge when we feel threatened or fearful. It wants only to survive at any cost. We downshift into our R-brain in settings that are unpredictable, disorderly, or threatening. We downshift in situations that lack boundaries and borders, where too many choices are present.

I was standing on a small platform attached to a tall redwood tree. Standing thirty-five feet below me, the other workshop participants were looking up and shouting to me; but I could not hear what they were saying. My knees were shaking. My breathing was shallow and irregular. I could not focus; everything seemed to spin around me. I felt frozen in space, my feet nailed to the platform. I had already accomplished what had seemed an impossible task. Climbing a tall redwood using cleats randomly nailed into the trunk, I had reached the platform on which I was standing.

I was now facing another, more difficult challenge. At the edge of the platform I saw a six-inch plank extending outward into space. My task was to walk to the end of this plank and jump toward a trapeze hanging ten feet away. Somewhere in my mind, I knew

I was perfectly safe. I had a helmet on my head. I was wearing a harness that went around my waist and shoulders. Attached to my harness was one end of a long, blue rope. Looking below, I could see a team of four people holding the other end of the rope. Their job was to make sure I remained safe at all times, even if I slipped or lost my balance and fell.

My thinking brain—my neocortex—understood that I was safe. But my R-brain was running the show. In fact, my R-brain was in overdrive. It knew only one thing: I was way too high in the air to be safe and I was about to walk a narrow plank and jump into thin air. No way was my R-brain going to let this catastrophe happen! My survival was at stake. I could feel the adrenaline coursing through my body. My heart rate was increasing and my muscles were tensing. I was in a full fight-flight response.

Under threatening or stressful conditions like this high-rope trapeze leap, we rapidly downshift into our R-brain, triggering our body's fight-flight response. This response, in turn, unleashes a number of chemical changes. It prompts an almost immediate drop in serotonin production. Serotonin is produced in the lower regions of the brainstem near the spinal cord. It makes possible the smooth transmission of electrochemical messages within the brain. Without sufficient serotonin, messages have difficulty leaping across the synapses, or gaps between cells, in the brain. People cannot think clearly or quickly when serotonin production is low. Thus, as I stood facing that trapeze, I could not focus my mind. I could not think what to do next.

Another chemical involved in downshifting is cortisol. Cortisol is produced in the adrenal glands as part of the fight-flight response. It travels quickly to the brain, where it does most of its work. High levels of cortisol damage brain structures and interrupt transmission of information from neuron to neuron. Such high levels of cortisol also make it difficult to think clearly. On that platform in the trees, I could hear the R-brain's mental chatter telling me I was in mortal danger. I was unable to think clearly about how to leap safely and successfully for the trapeze.

You do not have to be on a platform in a redwood forest to experience an R-brain downshift. What constitutes a threatening or stressful situation varies from person to person. Different degrees of downshifting occur because not all threats are experienced as equal. But the biochemical consequences of downshifting are predictable. When people downshift, their responses become more automatic and less thoughtful. They become less flexible and more rigid. They revert to familiar beliefs and behaviors even when these responses are dysfunctional. There is a narrowing of their perceptions, so they cannot read subtle environmental and internal cues.

Under almost any threatening or stressful condition, people's thinking capacity and problem-solving ability are severely impaired. Downshifting erodes our ability to access higher-order thinking. It reduces creativity and imagination. Thoughts become unclear and disjointed. Downshifting means we are less able to engage in complex tasks. We have more difficulty seeing interconnections and relationships. We overfocus on a single person or issue. We have a narrower view of the situation and a more limited set of responses.

In some cases, our response may be cold-blooded, reptilian aggression toward the source of the threat.

The competencies needed for human learning become least available when we downshift into the R-brain: the ability to think critically and creatively, the capacity for higher-order thinking, a wide perceptual field that recognizes new data, a willingness to explore unfamiliar ideas, values, or behaviors. When people are in a full R-brain downshift, they cannot learn. The R-brain is not open to "Aha!" moments that come suddenly to learners. Yet such moments are absolutely essential for faith formation and Christian teaching. Learning always involves being open to the unexpected. Lifelong learners expect new light and life to break forth from God's Word.

Learning means losing oneself, becoming vulnerable, risking oneself in relationships of care and concern. We will lose ourselves, our personal identity as we have known it, if we allow ourselves to grow. Powerful learning, therefore, almost automatically increases the possibility of downshifting. If we are downshifting, something important must be at stake. So we had better pay attention and dig deeper.

Christian sanctification or "going on to perfection" usually means letting go of old ways of thinking and acting so that we can embrace something more adequate, more true to the gospel. Learning something new, however, does not exist for the R-brain. Repentance and transformation are not in its vocabulary. The R-brain relies on precedent, habit, routine. An R-brain downshift deprives us of what we most need for Christian growth and transformation.

Many of our educational settings unintentionally contribute to an R-brain downshift. Imagine yourself in some urban classrooms where students and teachers live with high levels of threat to their personal safety. Consider some Sunday schools where the congregation feels under siege by a transitional neighborhood or where an intense church conflict is raging. Or picture a kindergartner's first day of Sunday school as she is left by her parents at the church door. Or what about a church school classroom that is cluttered, dingy, cramped, and uncomfortably hot or cold. All these situations can trigger an R-brain downshift.

Standing amid those redwood trees, I looked at the trapeze ahead of me. Suddenly I heard someone below shout: "Remember to breathe! Listen to the part of you that knows what to do!" So I took a deep breath. I consciously faced my R-brain's fears, broke through them, and jumped. Much to my surprise, my fingers grasped the trapeze. After that, I could hear the team's cheering and the sound of my own laughter. In a single instant, fear turned to joy.

Later, as I disconnected from my climbing belt, I wondered how often my R-brain's fears hold me back from life's laughter and joy, accomplishment and delight. How many times do I allow ten percent of my mind to exercise veto power over what the other ninety percent wants to do? Too often, I concluded. I had experienced the same involuntary downshift into fear and paralysis…

… when I walked into a room full of overactive junior high youth ready for a new year of UMYF;

... when someone in a study group began criticizing my interpretation of the Bible and questioning my faith;

... when a child in my Sunday school class spoke of her own pain and fear following her father's death in an auto accident;

... when I said "yes" to a project someone asked me to do and then realized I did not know where to begin;

... when the education committee's tense discussion of curriculum turned into an angry debate where harsh words and accusations hung in the air.

In many cases, our downshifting deprives us of joy. It drains us of our aliveness. It prevents us from playing full out with all God's gifts. It holds us back from the ministries to which God calls us. The shadow of the cross often falls across our choices. Following Jesus usually involves stepping out in faith, taking risks, stretching beyond our comfort zone. If we let our R-brain's fears hold us back, we never experience the joy of using our spiritual gifts at their full capacity. We never have the deep satisfaction of doing what God created us to do. We deprive ourselves of the transformative learning that sets us free from the past and makes us truly new creations in Christ.

Reversing the R-Brain Downshift. Paradoxically, the situations that cause us to downshift into our R-brain are the same situations that have the highest potential for learning and growth, for joy and delight. The possibilities for learning are greatest when our equilibrium is upset and we are confronted with new challenges, experiences, or information. In the very moments when we need the full capacity of the triune brain, the R-brain wants to downshift us into a paralyzing, fearful place.

Christian educators and church leaders foster deep learning when they recognize this R-brain downshift and develop strategies for managing it. Because basic chemical and involuntary processes drive the downshift phenomenon, we cannot change it by scolding or lecturing people on how they should feel or what they ought to do. Moralizing about right and wrong or preaching about love and peace cannot alter these biochemical changes. Such approaches may, in fact, be counterproductive. They only increase a sense of threat or fear. They accelerate our downshift into the R-brain.

What, then, can Christian educators do? First, we can be alert for an R-brain downshift in ourselves and others. Downshifting is a natural and automatic response to threatening situations. Teachers often forget that learning can be stressful. Exposure to new ideas or new behaviors may leave people awash in ambiguity and uncertainty. Such feelings are threatening and stressful. Our R-brain gremlins love the status quo. They like things just the way they are. These gremlins show up the most when they sense we are about to change, to grow, to be transformed. Being able consciously to name downshifting for what it is—a response to what the R-brain perceives as a threat to our survival—removes some of its power.

Like all mechanisms that work in the dark, downshifting's power is diminished when brought into the full light of awareness. One Sunday school teacher said: "I've learned to recognize when I'm starting to downshift and things are getting a little crazy. When that happens, I say to myself: 'O come on! There's no saber-toothed tiger around the bookcase. Let go of those fears and get on with it.' " Recognizing and naming an R-brain downshift undermines its ability to sabotage learning.

Second, teachers can design as much psychological safety into their classroom environments as possible. Hospitable space creates a safe climate for learning. Safe space minimizes downshifting into the R-brain. Opportunities for transformative Christian learning must always be accompanied by support and safety. Several strategies increase this sense of support and safety. Keep these strategies in mind:

- Set feasible goals for learning that are clear and understandable. When we are in a class but do not know what we are learning or why or how, we can feel threatened or confused.
- Set boundaries and norms for groups. Fuzzy boundaries or unclear norms can trigger an R-brain downshift.
- Discourage competition. Competition can trigger the R-brain's instinct for survival.
- Create a climate of mutual respect and affirmation.
- Show respect for each person.
- Ensure that the classroom is physically comfortable and the environment is calming.
- Work in small groups, helping learners feel they are cared for and important.
- Play calming music.
- Let learners know it is OK to make mistakes.

Third, practicing the means of grace minimizes the R-brain's impact on teaching and learning. Disciplines of prayer and meditation may not eliminate downshifting, but they can reduce its intensity and duration. People who practice the means of grace will downshift less deeply and will recover more quickly. Building the classic spiritual practices of prayer, Scripture reading, and meditation into both our personal lives and our classrooms buffers downshifting's destructive consequences.

Finally, invitations to higher-order thinking draw people out of their reptilian brains. Good questions are powerful tools for pulling people out of an R-brain downshift. Jesus' questions continually invited people to move from reactivity to response. "What do you want me to do for you?" he asks the man anxious and fearful about his health. He says to John's disciples, "What are you looking for?"

Powerful, open-ended questions challenge people to rise out of their anxious R-brains. They reconnect us to parts of the brain that are not driven by instinct and survival. A deeper wisdom becomes available when we move from the R-brain's survival instinct into the cortex's reason and imagination. Questions invite people to respond from their higher-order thinking rather than from their fears, from a place of creativity and not from an involuntary pattern.

Finally, our thinking becomes more inflexible and rigid when we downshift into our R-brain. Effective teaching encourages learners to invent options and entertain alternative possibilities. "Michelle, let's list ten different ways you could respond when you get angry with someone in the group," Mack said. Michelle, still red-faced and flustered, quickly named three or four possibilities. "Keep going," Mack said encouragingly. He recognized that these four options were just different ways of saying the same thing. By the time Michelle reached option eight, her thinking was beginning to shift. She was realizing she had actually thought of other possible ways to respond. She was shifting out of her reptilian brain back into her higher-order thinking.

Figure 2.4: Teacher Responses to an R-Brain Downshift

Downshifting Behaviors	Teacher Responses
Automatic Responses and "Knee-Jerk" Behaviors	Name Downshifting as It Is Happening and Do a Reality Check
Fight-Flight Response in Our Bodies	Practice Christian Hospitality Create Safe Space
"Cold-Blooded" Aggression or Out-of-Proportion Hostility	Practice Spiritual Disciplines
Thinking That Becomes Unclear, Disjointed	Invite Higher-Order Thinking Through Powerful Questions
Inflexible Thinking	Invent Options and Possibilities

The Limbic System

Wrapped around the brainstem is the limbic system. Composed of several structures roughly the size of olives or walnuts, the limbic system is the neural superhighway on which our emotions travel.[8] The limbic system's structures are loaded with peptides that allow them to communicate chemically with every cell in the body. Through these chemical mechanisms, the limbic system regulates our emotional pathways and priorities.

The limbic system's ability to generate strong emotions has both negative and positive consequences for faith formation [see Figure 2.5]. On one hand, strong emotions short-circuit our thinking and learning. They trigger chemical changes that alter our brains. Our brains become flooded with chemicals like cortisol that inhibit the passage of information from cell to cell. These changes make it difficult for us to think quickly and clearly. We have difficulty learning and remembering.

On the other hand, strong emotions enable powerful learning. Learning through our emotions is not the exception; it is the rule. Emotions play a vital role in our ability to think and to reason.[9]

When we experience an emotion, the cortex has a difficult time shutting it off or ignoring it. We can, after all, learn some things in spite of ourselves. My children often surprise me with what they remember from a fun-filled outing or field trip. The day's excitement and playfulness engender powerful learning. Without realizing it, they learn about animals and their habitats from a day at the zoo. Or they learn Christian ethical norms from a church camp's games and sports even though explicit moral instruction is not the goal.

Emotions focus our experience and learning. They grab our attention. Emotions tell the brain: Pay attention to this! They allow us quickly to identify the most important information in a complex environment. Learning and attentional focus are closely related. To learn something we must first focus on it. Without emotions, we lack the desire to focus our attention on something new.

Emotions also enhance our ability to maintain focus over time. We remember concepts and events that are emotionally laden. Because the brain gives preferential processing to emotions, the brain is highly stimulated in the presence of emotions. Emotions give learners a more activated and stimulated brain, which helps both initial processing and long-term memory. We can, for example, remember in great detail what we were doing when we first heard about a major national catastrophe such as Kennedy's assassination, the Challenger disaster, or September 11. The strong emotions we experienced in these moments powerfully embedded these memories in our minds.

Figure 2.5: The Role of Emotions in Learning

Negative Impact of Emotions	Positive Impact of Emotions
Trigger chemical changes that send us into fight/flight response and inhibit learning	Focus attention on what to learn
	Anchor new learning
	Make new learning memorable and more easily accessible to recall
	Override conscious resistance to learning
	Enhance creativity and imagination

Emotions are essential to vital Christian teaching and faith formation. Too often educators have treated learning and the emotions as opposites: Learning happens in the head; feelings reside in the heart. Worship touches our hearts; Sunday school is where we think about our beliefs.

The new science of the brain suggests we revise these assumptions. Without emotions we cannot think and learn. Emotions anchor learning. They make memories vivid and accessible. When parts of the brain's frontal lobes are removed because of tumor surgery, thinking skills are generally not significantly affected. But if surgeons remove parts of the limbic system, a patient's thinking is severely impaired.[10]

The limbic system reminds us that our brains always process emotions and information simultaneously. Thinking involves the whole self, not just the mind. Christian teaching and faith formation, at their best, do not compartmentalize learning. Loving God and knowing God, religious experience and doctrinal reflection belong together. They are not opposites. Emotions and thinking together foster true growth in Christ.

How the Limbic System Works. Each structure within the limbic system has a distinct function in processing information [see Figure 2.6]. Each plays a crucial role in Christian teaching and learning.

One of these structures is the thalamus. The thalamus serves as a relay and transfer station for sensory data arriving through the brainstem. It keeps the brain updated on what is happening in the outside world. Most of this information is forwarded to the cortex. In the cortex, it is processed and analyzed. The cortex may then decide to store some of this information in its memory.

To do this, the cortex sends messages to another organ in the limbic system: the hippocampus. The hippocampus is to the brain what a card catalog is to a library. Shaped like a sea horse, the hippocampus receives data from the cortex. It then catalogs memories and forwards them for storage in various parts of the brain. The hippocampus is like a switchboard for storing and accessing memories. The hippocampus does not develop until children are about three years old, which is why most people cannot remember events and people before that age.[11] Its late appearance also explains why Piaget noted that certain types of memory and reasoning develop only after age three.

Figure 2.6: How the Limbic System Processes Information

```
                                    ( Stimulus )
                                         |
                                         v
                                    ( Thalamus )
              Sorts & Stores             |
                    _____           v
                   /          \     ( Cortex )
      ( Hippocampus )          _____/
                   \          /
                    _____/
                   -- Receives --
```

Not all sensory data travels along this neural pathway from the thalamus to the cortex, however. A slender one-neuron link connects the thalamus to another part of the limbic system: the amygdala. About the size of a fingernail, it is connected to most areas of the brain. Unlike the hippocampus, which matures relatively late, the amygdala is fully formed early in our development. The amygdala processes and stores strong emotional memories.

It accounts for why we sometimes have a strong emotional response but cannot explain why we feel the way we do.[12] Our system for storing and retrieving emotions develops earlier than the rest of our memory system.

Emotion-laden data from the thalamus moves over this slender neural back alley to the amygdala. The amygdala then uses primitive categorizations to activate an immediate response. It receives only five percent or less of the total sensory information coming through the thalamus. The rest goes to the thinking brain, where it can be more thoroughly processed.[13] The amygdala is therefore always scanning foggy, fuzzy information and making snap judgments based upon it. These snap judgments are frequently wrong. Nonetheless, they have an immediate impact on our thinking and behaving.

This process worked wonderfully when we faced the danger of a stampeding woolly mammoth. It becomes dysfunctional in the modern world where mammoths and saber-toothed tigers are extinct. The amygdala causes us to overreact to minor threats. The subsequent emotional reactivity makes it difficult for the brain to think clearly. Based on limited data, the amygdala orchestrates a neural hijacking. It wreaks havoc on our ability to think clearly and respond calmly to everyday challenges and problems.[14]

If the amygdala encounters a sensory pattern similar to a powerful emotional memory, it responds immediately. The amygdala dimly sees a potential threat and says to itself, "Better be safe than sorry! I'm sending out the alarm." A message then goes to the hypothalamus. The hypothalamus contacts the pituitary gland, which sends chemical messages to the adrenal glands. They release adrenaline and other chemicals, such as cortisol. Blood rushes away from the digestive tract and to the legs and arms. The heartbeat increases so blood flows more rapidly to the muscles, preparing them to fight or run. As a fight-flight response floods the body, thinking capacity drops. We sink into an R-brain downshift. In short, a neural hijacking in our limbic system triggers an R-brain downshift [see Figure 2.7].

Figure 2.7: A Neural Hijacking

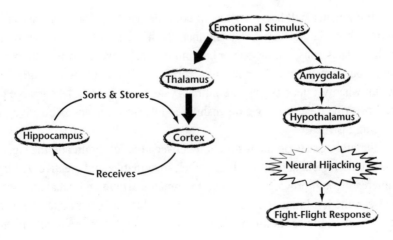

Stopping a Neural Hijacking. When we resist learning, this resistance usually does not lie in our thoughts. It comes from our emotions. Resistance is ultimately an emotional phenomenon, not a logical one. Strong emotions—a neural hijacking—make it nearly impossible to break through resistance.

Martha enjoys singing in her church's teen choir. She particularly liked Enrique, the former choir director who recently resigned. But she has no such positive feelings for the new director, Jack. Jack's gestures and tone of voice remind Martha of her father, who is always critical of her. At last night's rehearsal Jack said, "I don't think the sopranos have their part down. Let's go over it again." Martha felt her stomach tighten. An uncontrollable rage boiled up in her. Before she knew what was happening, she snapped back angrily, "Why don't you sing it yourself if we aren't good enough." A few moments later, she apologized to Jack. "I don't know what came over me. I just wasn't myself, I guess," she said.

Jack triggered Martha's amygdala. Picking up fuzzy and out-of-focus signals in Jack's words and tone of voice, Martha's amygdala immediately searched its storehouse of negative emotional memories and found a match: her critical father. Martha experienced a neural hijacking. Her hot amygdala impaired her ability to turn off a negative thought or feeling. It flooded her body with cortisol and other fight-flight chemicals, further disrupting her ability to respond calmly to Jack's comments.

The limbic system can short-circuit our best thinking and learning. We cannot learn in the midst of a neural hijacking. The brain, flooded with chemicals that wreak havoc with our neural networks, cannot concentrate. It becomes agitated. It drops into either/or thinking and worst-case scenarios. It lashes out angrily at others. Emotional reactivity is like turning on the radio and getting static rather than music.

The real problem, however, is that the cortex thinks it is still driving the car when the limbic system and R-brain are actually doing the steering. Our cortex is working in service of the limbic system and R-brain. Our thinking is distorted, emotionally charged, regressive.

A driver-training car will have two sets of controls. The driver has one set of brakes and a steering wheel. The instructor has another, duplicate set of controls. If the student does something dangerous, the instructor can immediately take control of the vehicle. In the same way, our cortex normally does the steering. We are thinking logically, rationally, creatively. But when we get anxious, the limbic system and R-brain take charge of the controls and override the cortex. We downshift, and the result is not as positive as it is with the driving instructor.

A lot of literature exists on the distinction between the left brain and the right brain. One hemisphere is logical and rational; the other, imaginative and creative. All this research is interesting and provides insights into human learning and behavior. But the difference between the left brain and right brain is much less important than the distinction between the upper and lower brain, between the cortex and the R-brain with its ally the limbic system.

The most important thing we can do in the midst of a neural hijacking is to breathe deeply and do nothing. The word *emotion* comes from the Latin *emovere,* which literally means to move out. Emotions have an outward thrust. The limbic system's strong emotions prompt us to take immediate action. This response made sense for our ancestors who faced everyday dangers in the natural world. Now, however, it causes us to treat everyday difficulties as if they were life-threatening attacks. The result is a state of chronically having our minds hijacked by our fears and anxieties.

According to some authors, a quarter-second gap exists between the time the brain sends an impulse to act and the time the body starts to obey this signal. The human will resides in this gap.[15] In this quarter-second gap, we can choose whether or not to act. The key to preventing a neural hijacking lies in breaking the quarter-second link between emotion and action. Strategies such as posing powerful questions, counting to ten, or taking a deep breath can break this link. These strategies allow the cortex to regain its perspective. It gives the thinking brain some breathing room to examine the other 95 percent of sensory information that went to it rather than to the amygdala.

The Christian tradition of spiritual discernment contains important clues for handling a neural hijacking. Discernment encourages an attitude of indifference. We choose not to act on an impulse. Resting in a place of indifference, we test the spirits. What is really moving us to action? Do our impulses come from a good spirit or an evil one? Do they come from a fuzzy, out-of-focus panic attack in the amygdala? What about the other 95 percent of the information our thinking mind is processing? "Beloved, do not believe every spirit, but test the spirits to see whether they are from God" (1 John 4:1). Practicing spiritual discernment trains us for the habit of holy indifference, which militates against a neural hijacking.

Using the Limbic System's Emotions to Maximize Learning. The limbic system does more than simply short-circuit learning by triggering a neural hijacking. It can also enhance learning.

What fuels our learning and growing as Christians? It is more than logic and reason. Emotions are absolutely essential for powerful, deep learning. We become what we love and that is how we grow. Behind all learning lies a deeper desire, a more profound longing:

> As a deer longs for flowing streams,
>   so my soul longs for you, O God.
> My soul thirsts for God,
>   for the living God.
>
> Psalm 42:1-2

Our emotions, our longings and desires, ultimately fuel our growth in Christ.

Our emotions are the distillation of learned wisdom. Life's critical survival lessons are hardwired into our emotions. Making decisions based on our emotions is not an exception. It is the rule. For nearly three hundred years, the Western world has thought that the frontal lobes—reasoning and logic—generate our best thoughts. "I think, therefore I am," concluded Descartes. The neocortex may indeed create our best thoughts and plans. But the limbic system's emotions really trigger and drive them.

Jonathan could not remember having such a good time. His Sunday school teacher had divided the class into teams. Each team was given a different biblical passage and asked to develop a skit to share with the rest of the class. Working with his friends, Jonathan was amazed at how easily ideas began to flow after some initial awkwardness. Jonathan felt a little nervous when his group stood up and performed their skit. But his stage fright quickly gave way to laughter and a sense of accomplishment. He was surprised at how well each team did. One of the skits made him laugh. A year later, Jonathan still remembers those Bible stories.

Jonathan's experience illustrates the limbic system's power to enhance learning. His teacher harnessed powerful emotions to focus and deepen learning. While the limbic system can conduct a neural hijacking, it can also create feelings of playfulness, emotional closeness, and joy. These feelings are essential for effective Christian teaching and learning. Emotions motivate us to learn. They enhance our ability to remember. They focus our attention.

Christian educators can use strong emotions to focus attention, learning, and memory. The limbic system is a powerful ally in Christian teaching and faith formation. Several strategies help to harness the limbic system for effective learning [see Figure 2.8].

First, the human brain gives preferential processing to emotion-laden experiences. The more emotions are aroused, the stronger the memory. The stronger the memory, the more deeply memories are imprinted. Emotions thus stimulate the brain's most powerful learning.

Feeling and thinking are not two separate spheres. They work together in the service of learning. Teachers harness the limbic system when they appreciate the role of feelings and emotions in teaching. A classroom's emotional climate and mood speak immediately to the limbic system. Candles, posters, banners, colorful bulletin boards, and other symbols create an emotional tone that enhances and supports learning. Music and song also evoke an emotional response.

Tonya came early on Sunday morning to arrange her classroom. Earlier in the week she had reviewed her lesson. She created a bulletin board using Sunday school pictures and reproductions of art classics that depicted the passage they were studying. With an eye for form and texture, she thumbtacked these items on the walls. Tonya began her lesson with singing. The songs were lively and got her students using their whole bodies. She even had them stand and move to the music, making hand motions and dancing across the room. The songs' images bridged into Tonya's lesson. By the time her sixth-grade students were reading the Scripture lesson, their emotions were focused and ready to make connections. They were ready to learn and remember.

Second, teachers can use physical and emotional focal points to anchor learning. These focal points stimulate deeper interaction with the material. Soo-Jin placed two stuffed animals in the middle of her table. She asked her first-grade Sunday school class: "What does Paul say in today's Scripture lesson that reminds us how being a Christian is like being a teddy bear? Like being a giraffe?" She divided the class into two groups. The teddy bears generated as many answers as they could to this question. The giraffes did the same. After writing their answers on the dry-erase board, Soo-Jin launched into her lesson. She returned throughout the lesson to her physical focal point of the two stuffed animals. Months later, her students could still remember how Paul said being a Christian was like being a giraffe.

Music can also be an emotional focal point that anchors Christian faith formation. Matt played a brief excerpt from a popular song at the beginning of his senior high class. Then he said: "There's a strong message in this song. What did you hear as you listened to it?" Throughout his lesson, Matt would stop and play the song again. The song served as an emotional anchor for learning.

Physical and emotional focal points stimulate the limbic system. But they are not subtle teaching strategies. Teachers may want to tell learners what they are doing with a focal point. It is also important to return repeatedly to the focal point so it becomes an emotional touchstone for the whole class period.

Third, cooperative and collaborative learning activities harness the limbic system's emotional power. Group activities stimulate playfulness and warm, interpersonal close-ness. These feelings bring attentional focus to learning. Collaboration can take several forms. It can occur among students. Soo-Jin had two groups—teddy bears and giraffes—generate possible answers. Jonathan's teacher divided her class into groups who presented different skits. The lesson is better remembered because emotions of playfulness and rela-tional closeness are associated with the content.

Another form of collaboration occurs between the teacher and students. In many adult classes, the teacher is a facilitator who helps release participants into inquiry and discov-ery. Unfortunately, some teachers need to be the final authority, thus inhibiting group sharing that could activate limbic emotions and enhance learning.

Finally, ritual activates the limbic system. At the end of every junior high Sunday school class, LaVon asks students to stand in a circle, facing the back of the student ahead of them. She then says, "Raise your left hand to lock in all the ways you came to know God today." And the students raise their left hands into the middle of the circle. Then she says: "Lower your right hand to lock in all the ways you came to love God today." And they lower their right arms out into the space beyond the circle. LaVon next commands them: "Lift your left foot to lock in all the ways you committed yourself to serve God today." They lift their left feet into the circle, balancing on one foot.

Then she shouts: "Slap'em and clap'em! Let's lock it all in!" Immediately they all bring their hands together in a loud clap and snap their feet together on the floor. Then they turn into the circle and face each other, still holding their hands in a gesture of prayer, and together say "God be with you this week." This weekly ritual is a powerful experience for LaVon's students. It helps them "lock in the learning" for the week.

Figure 2.8: Strategies for Activating the Limbic System in Learning

Strategy	Example
Stop a Neural Hijacking	• Take a deep breath before acting/speaking • Count to ten before acting/speaking • Pose higher-order questions to self/others • Practice holy indifference
Create a Mood or Feeling Climate	• Candles • Posters • Banners
Use Music and Song	• Dance • Creative movement • Singing
Use a Physical or Emotional Focal Point	• Object returned to throughout the lesson (teddy bear, giraffe, candle, open Bible) • A song or piece of music played several times throughout the lesson
Use the Power of Play and Bonding	• Collaborative learning in groups • Group activities • Games
Incorporate Ritual	• Opening or closing rituals • Prayer

THE CEREBRUM AND NEOCORTEX

The cerebrum and neocortex constitute the newest and uniquely human portion of the brain. Thought and speech, learning and memory, planning and decision-making reside here. Two thirds of the brain's mass consists of the cerebrum's twin hemispheres. Covering them is the neocortex. The neocortex is a many-folded sheet of tissue about an eighth of an inch thick. Spread flat, it would cover about one and one-half square feet.[16] Its twisted, multiple folds give the neocortex the appearance of woody bark. Hence its name: the word *cortex* means bark.

Distributed Processing of Information. The brain's twin hemispheres house our sensory and thinking capacities. Our sensory processing is not concentrated in any single section of the brain but is scattered throughout it. Part of the frontal lobe called Broca's area helps us form spoken words. Visual information is lodged in an area at the back of the brain. The areas located on the sides of the brain nearest to the ears house auditory data. Touch and motor control are concentrated in an area near the top of the head.

The distributed nature of sensory processing means that something as simple as listening to a friend is actually an amazingly complicated activity. The brain is retrieving, synthesizing, and processing sensory data from multiple places simultaneously. Separate neural pathways bring sensory data from our eyes, ears, nose, or skin to different areas of the brain. Some pathways register tone of voice; others, facial expression. Still others handle gesture or smell. The brain almost instantaneously combines these sensory messages, searching for meaningful patterns. We listen effortlessly to our friend, unaware of the tremendous complexity occurring within our brains.

This processing of information means that thinking is not a linear process of matching item A in the world with item B in the brain. It is not like a letter moving through the post office, going from one bin to the next. It is more like the lights on a theater marquee. An MRI scan would show that many parts of the brain light up with activity when we are thinking or remembering. As different sensory messages crisscross the brain, the brain looks for patterns. The brain's interconnectivity predisposes it to search for connections and patterns. It generates new patterns from incomplete signals. It matches incoming sensory data with existing patterns. As a result of this complex activity, we think and learn.

Learning and Memory Engage the Whole Brain. The same complex process occurs when we remember something. As I walked into the kitchen yesterday, I smelled freshly baked cookies. Smelling them, I remembered my grandmother's kitchen. I saw the rocking chair by the window, the calendar pinned to the wall, my grandfather's coat hanging near the door, the plants arranged in the south window.

Where is this memory of my grandmother's kitchen? My brain does not have a file drawer neatly labeled "cookies baking in grandmother's kitchen, 1967." Instead, many places scattered throughout the brain work together to store and retrieve this memory. Memory, like thinking, is distributed across the brain [see Figure 2.9]. Activating a memory sends signals flashing to many parts of the brain, from which various elements are retrieved, combined, and rehearsed.

Memory is a process, not a place. This is why forgotten facts come to us

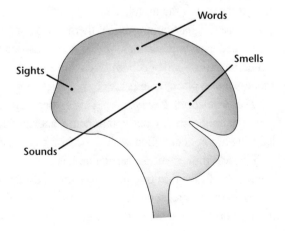

Figure 2.9: Thinking About My Grandmother's Kitchen

hours after we stopped trying to remember them. Some parts of the brain kept searching scattered circuits and associational links until they connected to the desired data. When one bit of data was recovered, it led to the other interconnected pieces. Suddenly the information leapt into our awareness. Memory is a giant spider web where every piece of information is connected in multiple ways. Touch one part of the web and it activates all the other links.

The more neural pathways activated when a memory is created, the easier it is to remember. The more sensory channels used in learning, the more powerful the learning. We more easily forget experiences that do not engage multiple sensory channels. We remember those that do. If teachers give verbal instructions on how to do something, students forget them within a few hours. If they give both verbal instructions and a demonstration, students remember them much longer. Why? Because more sensory channels are used and more parts of the brain activated. The pattern is more widespread so the neural connections are more complex.

Powerful learning and rich memories weave a vivid tapestry of neural associations. They require the stimulation of multiple sensory channels. I remember clearly the day I was baptized as a young adult. This memory serves as a touchstone for my Christian life. It is a powerful memory because so many sensory channels were working to form a densely connected pattern of meaning: the sound and feel of water, the sweet smell of wine, the yeasty aroma of bread, the physical movement to the front of the church, the words spoken, the beeswax candles, the sound of singing, the emotions of awe, commitment, and acceptance.

Effective faith formation involves more than listening quietly to talking heads. It engages all the senses. It lays down a spider web of interconnected meanings, which are powerfully stored and retrieved from many parts of the brain.

Jennifer's age group studies the same Scripture passage for four weeks. One week they engage in a craft related to the passage's theme. The following week, they create a skit based on the lesson and videotape it. They read and discuss the passage on the next Sunday. At the end of the month, Jennifer and her classmates have used many parts of the brain to explore this particular biblical theme or passage. Multiple sensory channels have been stimulated, weaving a spider web of neural associations that make it easier for Jennifer to remember. Her Sunday school leaders are honoring the discovery that remembering is a process, not a place; a spider web, not a file bin.

The Brain-Body Connection. This spider web of memory is not limited to our three-pound brain. It actually has components that run throughout the whole body.[17] Memory and learning are not contained within the iron cage of the mind. They extend into the body.

Physical movement, in particular, has a close connection to learning and memory. The same part of the brain that processes the body's physical movement also processes and stores learning.[18] Jensen cites studies suggesting that people who exercise seventy-five minutes or more per week show quicker physical reactions, think more clearly, and have more rapid memories. Just as physical exercise strengthens muscles and lungs, it also strengthens the cerebellum and other key areas of the brain.

Christianity is the most material of religions. It takes the physical body seriously. God became flesh in Jesus Christ and thus every physical body is sacred. Christian educators have long understood the importance of physical movement to learning. Many transformative religious rituals incorporate physical movement. In receiving the Eucharist, for example, people walk, cup their hands, eat, drink, kneel, and engage in other physical postures of prayer. Baptism too is a physical, embodied experience.

The brain-body connection suggests that Christian education involves more than sitting in a chair. Physical movement can anchor learning. Learners can be taught to access memories and emotions by assuming a particular posture or stance.

Too many congregations complain about the free movement of children through halls or across the fellowship hall during coffee hour. Perhaps their running, dancing, skipping, and playing are more than random gestures. They are not "just blowing off steam" or have not "eaten too many cookies." Physical movement is critical for learning. When we deprive children of ways to intentionally link brain and body, they will invent their own ways to do so. How much more powerful could our Christian education become if we found ways to harness physical movement more intentionally and creatively in the service of Christian faith formation?

A LIQUID BRAIN

Our quick tour of the triune brain leaves some questions unanswered: How do the various parts of our triune brain communicate? What pathways do they use to weave together this spider web of knowing and remembering?

A Smooth Path Through a Neural Forest. To communicate with each other, neurons need to send and receive information. Every neuron has two kinds of extensions designed to do this. One extension—called a dendrite—receives information. The other—called an axon—sends information. A tiny gap (called a synapse) exists between these extensions. Neurons use chemical molecules called neurotransmitters to bridge this gap. Neurotransmitters code the information they process, taking it from one neuron's axon to another's dendrite. Like a key placed into a lock, if the neurotransmitter sent from one neuron's axon connects to another's dendrite, the door opens. Information jumps the gap or synapse between the two cells.[19]

Chemical neurotransmitters are thus essential for communication between neurons. They make thinking, feeling, and remembering possible. Scientists have identified more than fifty different neurotransmitters, including chemicals called peptides. They play a crucial role within the brain. Without them, neurons could not communicate. Medical research is discovering how levels of different neurotransmitters may be responsible for everything from attention deficit disorder to depression.

Even small changes in these chemical neurotransmitters can affect the brain's ability to think, learn, and remember. When we drop into our R-brain, changes in these chemical neurotransmitters affect our ability to think and reason. They make it difficult for neurons in different parts of the brain to communicate rapidly.

Use It or Lose It. When neurons communicate frequently, their dendrites grow additional receptor sites. These receptor sites increase the speed of transmission across the synapses.[20] As a result, the brain works more quickly and efficiently. When Robert first learned to play the piano, his fingers responded slowly to the notes that his eyes were reading on the page. As he practiced, neural pathways between certain cells grew stronger. More receptor sites were formed. Messages between neurons moved more rapidly. Consequently, Robert's fingers now move effortlessly across the keyboard.

Frequent activation of the same pattern causes physical changes in the brain that strengthen some neural pathways. The stronger the pathway, the more rapidly the sensory information moves along it. For this reason, we can remember a familiar face, address, or telephone number more easily than an unfamiliar one.

As the brain's neurons communicate and connect, some synapses are strengthened while others decay. Some brain pathways grow stronger and faster; others are lost entirely. Behind our house is a wooded hillside. When we first moved to our farm, this hillside was choked with brambles and weeds. The brush was so thick we could not walk through it. Eventually we cut a path through the woods. Our first path was narrow and uneven. It was barely wide enough for us to saunter single-file along it. As we walked this path over the years, it became wider and smoother. In the same way, neural networks become wider and smoother with use. These neural superhighways are important for human learning. Learning involves the brain's capacity to retrieve data rapidly and to communicate efficiently. Just as a muscle grows stronger with exercise, so our neural pathways grow stronger with use.

In the first year of life, we produce these neurons and their connections at an amazing rate. In the womb, the embryo generates new brain cells at a rate of 250,000 per minute or 15 million per hour. At birth, the brain weighs only one pound. It doubles to two pounds by our first birthday. It then grows more slowly until it reaches its final weight of three pounds during our late teens.[21]

This growth pattern explains why early stimulation and play are so important for learning. If the brain does not develop a rich, complex pattern of neural pathways during infancy, cultivating this capacity later in life is difficult. Christian educators are rightly concerned with the early religious experiences of infants and toddlers. During these years, the brain is structuring itself. It is laying down the neural pathways by which it will learn and make meaning across the lifespan.

One substance that helps these neural pathways fire more rapidly is myelin. Myelin acts like insulation, coating the neuron's axon and allowing messages to travel quickly. Myelin begins coating our neurons at birth and is released in stages. It begins in the lower brain and spreads, usually by adolescence, to the prefrontal cortex, where higher-order thinking resides. But just as some children grow faster or enter puberty more quickly than others, some brains produce myelin more rapidly than others. The result is that some children acquire higher-order thinking skills sooner than others.[22]

When Sunday school teachers demand higher-order moral or religious thinking of their youngest students, they may be asking them to do something for which their brains are not yet prepared. Children's readiness for religion may be rooted in brain development, not in motivation or interest.

Our Custom-Built Brain. While the human brain is strengthening some neural pathways, others are being pruned away. Some neural pathways grow stronger; others shrink. Seldom used connections decay and disappear. The human brain begins with billions of potential neural pathways. But a growing child's experience and environment strengthen some pathways and extinguish others. The brain is customized to each person's particular experiences.

"Train children in the right way, and when old, they will not stray," advises the Book of Proverbs (Proverbs 22:6). Experiences in early childhood—when the brain is laying down its fundamental hardscape of neural pathways—are absolutely critical for how children will later appropriate the Christian faith. Rich experiences with art and music, for example, lay down the creativity and imagination so critical for mature Christian experience. Patterns of prayer and meditation can be introduced much earlier in a child's life than we might suppose, particularly if these early experiences shape the brain's emerging neural architecture.

Howard Gardner proposes that intelligence is too complex to measure with a single number on an IQ test. Instead, he identifies at least seven types of intelligence. These range from linguistic intelligence to spatial intelligence, from musical intelligence to bodily-kinesthetic intelligence.[23] These different intelligences may reflect the neural pruning and branching that customize the human brain early in life.

Every human brain is absolutely unique. Neural pruning and branching explain why some people use a screwdriver with surgical precision but others are all thumbs. Some people recognize patterns in music while others hear only a cacophony of instruments. Some people move effortlessly on the dance floor but others stumble over their own feet.

Our gifts and talents have their origins in how the growing brain customizes itself, making each of us an absolutely unique individual. Just as a master vinegrower prunes some branches so the vine bears much fruit, experience and environment strengthen some neural pathways and prune others so our lives will bear abundant fruit (John 15:1-17). The origins of our differing spiritual gifts may lie in the brain's early neural pruning and branching.

Christian educators have an opportunity to stretch underutilized networks. Neural pruning may customize our brains to work efficiently, but it also limits our thinking and imagination. If the brain is predisposed to think along certain well-worn pathways, we can fall into the trap of responding habitually and automatically to life. If we always rehearse the same few biblical themes and beliefs, then we may lose the ability to conceptualize the gospel in other ways. If worship creates a neural predisposition for a particular type of music or participation, we may conclude that God is absent from other styles. Staying in our spiritual comfort zone is not just a matter of habit; it is also rooted in how we inadvertently customize our neural pathways. We end up with a God who is too small because we have pruned too closely the synapses of our brains.

Brainwork for the Mind

Just as we use exercise to build muscle tissue, we need "brainwork" to strengthen underused synapses. Cardellichio and Field propose seven strategies for neural branching [see Figure 2.10].[24] These strategies enrich neural networks and broaden interconnectivity within the brain. They create opportunities for people to stretch beyond their well-worn neural pathways.

Hypothetical Thinking. By requiring us to think about familiar things in unexpected ways, hypothetical thinking stimulates neural branching. For example,
- What would have happened if Paul had gone to Africa rather than Greece?
- If Luther had never begun the Reformation, how would the church look today?

The key to hypothetical thinking is not merely to ask questions outside the standard answers. Its power lies in posing follow-up questions that illuminate the complexity of events and ideas.

Reversal. One specific type of hypothetical thinking is reversal, which highlights particular components of a situation by reversing the perspective. When my sons were small, we would work on visual puzzles. Trying to find a hidden object, we would turn the picture upside down to see if another angle of vision helped us find it. Reversal strategies rely on this same technique. For example,
- What if the Jerusalem Council had decided all Christians had to accept circumcision and kosher laws?
- What would American religion be like if the British had won the Revolutionary War?

Applying a Different Symbol System. We typically use a particular language to describe faith experiences. What would happen if we described our faith using a different symbol system? At a recent retreat, the leader took each verse of a psalm and asked a participant to adopt a physical pose expressing its meaning. The whole psalm was then physically embodied down the middle of the room. This physical embodiment produced a different response from merely reading the psalm in unison. The retreat leader invited participants to experience the psalm through a different symbol system and, in doing so, opened up a new depth of meaning for everyone.

Analogy. Analogies require people to think outside their usual patterns. They require people to make connections between parts of their brains usually kept separate. As a result, underutilized neural pathways are stretched and strengthened. For example,
- If we were comparing the experience of faith to different types of fruits and vegetables, what would prevenient, justifying, and sanctifying grace be?
- How are different churches like different kinds of cars?

Figure 2.10: Strategies for Brainwork

Brainwork Strategy	Definition
Hypothetical Thinking	Ask "What-if" questions.
Reversal	Look at an idea or event from another perspective that reverses the familiar situation.
Applying a Different Symbol System	Describe a belief, idea, or concept using a different symbol system. For example, use artwork rather than words to depict the Trinity or use movement and music rather than words to describe the crucifixion.
Analogy	Ask students to compare something familiar to something unfamiliar or unusual and see what they discover.
Analyzing Points of View	Ask students to examine an idea or event from the perspective of someone different from themselves.
Completion	Ask students to fill in the gaps in incomplete information with reasonable guesses they can explain or justify.
Web Analysis	Ask students to identify as many complex effects as they can from one event.

- If you were to compare church leadership to a pair of shoes, what kind of shoes would it be?

Analyzing Points of View. Asking people to think about a person, event, or idea from another point of view encourages them to exercise unfamiliar neural pathways. For example,

- What would a Muslim say about this? A Buddhist?
- How would someone who is totally unfamiliar with the Bible interpret this passage?
- How many different ways can you explain what we mean by grace?

Completion. Our minds naturally wonder what is missing when we see something incomplete. To complete the missing piece, our brains search neglected pathways for information and connections. In the process, neural networks are stretched and strengthened. In using this strategy, participants must be guided toward answers that are reasonable. They must also be encouraged to provide multiple options so they think more flexibly. For example,

- If we had only a call to worship and a benediction, what could we do between them?
- If we did not have the book of Acts, how would we explain what happened between the gospels and Paul's letters?

Web Analysis. Hypothetical thinking generates multiple answers. Web analysis tries to uncover complex effects flowing from a single source. It stimulates neural branching by looking beyond the obvious answers. Web analysis challenges us to see the world around us in a new way. For example,

- How many lives were affected in what ways because John Wesley participated in the Holy Club at Oxford?
- What are the effects of the decision that the Bible could be translated into languages other than Greek and Hebrew?

Jesus and Neural Branching. Early in our cognitive development, the brain customizes itself to respond quickly and efficiently to familiar environmental triggers. Neural pruning and branching allow the brain to accomplish many things effortlessly and quickly. They also cause us to become victims of self-imposed limits on our thinking. If Christian conversion involves a new way of seeing the world, then it has something to do with neural pruning and branching. Putting on the mind of Christ entails stretching beyond the well-worn neural pathways of the old self.

Throughout his ministry Jesus used analogies to stretch his hearers' neural pathways. He told his listeners that the reign of God is like a mustard seed, a lost coin, or a treasure buried in a field. He invited his listeners to fill ambiguous gaps, asking "Whose image is on this coin?" His parables looked at life from alternative points of view. They reversed conventional religious values and invited people to enter an alternative symbolic universe. Modern neuroscience gives us a new appreciation for ancient Christian practices. It provides insights into how church educators can foster transformative Christian teaching and faith formation.

Conclusion

The new science of the brain thus leads us back to ancient patterns of Christian teaching and learning. Keeping in touch with recent discoveries in teaching and brain research guides us toward Christian teaching and faith formation that

- integrate the heart with the mind and soul;
- value the emotions and their role in faith formation;
- create a hospitable, welcoming climate that minimizes the potential for an R-brain downshift;
- balance challenge with support, and change with stability;
- set the practice of spiritual disciplines at the center of faith formation;

- teach by asking powerful questions that invite higher-order thinking;
- use celebrations, rituals, music, art, and other media to harness the power of the emotions;
- incorporate opportunities for cooperative and collaborative learning into the classroom, especially skits, roleplay, and simulations;
- see the learning potential of play and playfulness;
- bring the whole body into the classroom, not just the head;
- challenge people to examine familiar mental maps in imaginative, novel, and new ways for the sake of transformative growth in Christ;
- possess a tolerance for ambiguity, trusting that God's truth emerges only out of diversity and difference.

Christian educators can learn much from the new science of the brain. They can also learn from thinkers and writers who have tried to understand how the brain's cognitive development influences teaching, learning, and faith formation. It is to these thinkers that we now turn.

Deepening Your Learning

1. When was the last time you experienced an R-brain downshift? Describe this incident and explore what it suggests about the environments or relationships you create as a Sunday school teacher, small-group leader, or committee chairperson.

2. Describe a recent neural hijacking. What were the triggers? How did you react? Recover? What can you learn from this experience to create more powerful learning environments?

3. Design a lesson plan in which you only use the seven strategies for neural branching [see Figure 2.10]. How is this lesson similar to the way you usually teach? What would happen if you taught like this more often?

4. Try using your body to access different memories or feelings. For example, put yourself in a physical posture of bending down and curling in on yourself and then try describing something you are happy and excited about. Or stand with your chest flung forward and your arms outspread and your head high. Then try talking about something that depresses you or makes you sad. How does your posture affect your mood? Your feelings? Your thoughts? What does this experience suggest about ways you could use posture and physical movement in your teaching?

ENDNOTES

1 See *A Celebration of Neurons: An Educator's Guide to the Human Brain,* by Robert Sylwester (Association for Supervision and Curriculum Development, 1995), page 1.

2 See *Teaching With the Brain in Mind,* by Eric Jensen (Association for Supervision and Curriculum Development, 1998), pages 8, 10.

3 See *Teaching With the Brain in Mind,* by Eric Jensen (Association for Supervision and Curriculum Development, 1998), page 10.

4 See "To Be Intelligent," by John Abbott, in *Educational Leadership,* Vol. 54, no. 6, March 1997; page 7.

5 See *Teaching With the Brain in Mind,* by Eric Jensen (Association for Supervision and Curriculum Development, 1998), page 11; and *A Celebration of Neurons: An Educator's Guide to the Human Brain,* by Robert Sylwester (Association for Supervision and Curriculum Development, 1995), page 1.

6 See *Teaching With the Brain in Mind,* by Eric Jensen (Association for Supervision and Curriculum Development, 1998), page 83.

7 See *Making Connections: Teaching and the Human Brain,* by Renate Nummela Caine and Geoffrey Caine (Association for Supervision and Curriculum Development, 1991), page 64.

8 See *Teaching With the Brain in Mind,* by Eric Jensen (Association for Supervision and Curriculum Development, 1998), page 73.

9 See *Descartes' Error: Emotion, Reason, and the Human Brain,* by Antonio R. Damasio (Quill/Harper-Collins, 1995).

10 See *Teaching With the Brain in Mind,* by Eric Jensen (Association for Supervision and Curriculum Development, 1998), page 75.

11 See *Learning and Memory: The Brain in Action,* by Marilee Sprenger (Association for Supervision and Curriculum Development, 1999), page 55.

12 See *Emotional Intelligence,* by Daniel Goleman (Bantam Books, 1995), pages 16-24.

13 See *Emotional Alchemy: How the Mind Can Heal the Heart,* by Tara Bennett-Goleman (Three Rivers Press, 2001), page 135.

14 See *Emotional Intelligence,* by Daniel Goleman (Bantam Books, 1995), pages 16-24.

15 See *Emotional Alchemy: How the Mind Can Heal the Heart,* by Tara Bennett-Goleman (Three Rivers Press, 2001), page 179.

16 See *The Three-Pound Universe,* by Judith Hooper and Dick Teresi (Jeremy P. Tarcher, 1986), pages 36-37.

17 See *Teaching With the Brain in Mind,* by Eric Jensen (Association for Supervision and Curriculum Development, 1998), page 100.

18 See *Teaching With the Brain in Mind,* by Eric Jensen (Association for Supervision and Curriculum Development, 1998), pages 83-86.

19 See *A Celebration of Neurons: An Educator's Guide to the Human Brain,* by Robert Sylwester (Association for Supervision and Curriculum Development, 1995), page 35.

20 See *A Celebration of Neurons: An Educator's Guide to the Human Brain,* by Robert Sylwester (Association for Supervision and Curriculum Development, 1995), pages 88-91.

21 See *Teaching With the Brain in Mind,* by Eric Jensen (Association for Supervision and Curriculum Development, 1998), page 19; and *A Celebration of Neurons: An Educator's Guide to the Human Brain,* by Robert Sylwester (Association for Supervision and Curriculum Development, 1995), page 128.

22 See *Learning and Memory: The Brain in Action,* by Marilee Sprenger (Association for Supervision and Curriculum Development, 1999), pages 5-7.

23 See *Frames of Mind: The Theory of Multiple Intelligences,* by Howard Gardner (Basic Books, 1983).

24 See "Seven Strategies That Encourage Critical Thinking," by Thomas Cardellichio and Wendy Field, in *Educational Leadership,* Vol. 54, no. 6, March 1997; pages 33-36.

CHAPTER THREE

Growing in Wisdom and Maturity

Jean Piaget and Developmental Theory

Visit almost any Sunday school classroom in North America and you will find graded curriculum. Browse through catalogs selling Sunday school resources and you see graded curriculum. Graded materials are almost universally used in religious education. "Graded" refers to the concept that classroom curriculum is age appropriate. Each age group or grade level has a lesson suitable for its unique physical, mental, and cognitive abilities. Kindergarten materials are written differently than junior high resources. Second-graders and sixth-graders do not share the same lesson plans.

A major accomplishment of twentieth-century religious educators has been the preparation and widespread adoption of graded Sunday school materials. Researchers carefully studied childhood's developmental stages. Curriculum writers used these observations to produce a comprehensive array of graded Sunday school resources. Denominations promoted these materials and encouraged their adoption. As a result, many Sunday school leaders and teachers would never consider using anything but graded curriculum.

Behind these efforts is a fundamental insight: Our awareness, understanding, and thinking change as we grow. Children are not small-sized adults. A child's body is not the same as an adult's body. Nor is a child's brain the same as an adult's brain. Childhood reasoning follows a different logic than adult thinking. Even within childhood, mental operations evolve over time.

This insight is a relatively recent development. Throughout most of human history, adults viewed children as small versions of themselves. The next time you visit a museum, wander through its portrait collections. If you look at paintings of children before the late 1800's, they are usually portrayed as small-sized adults. They frequently have adult-looking heads placed atop pint-sized bodies. Until recently, children were generally regarded in this way. Children might grow physically; but their thinking, reasoning, and feeling were the same as adult thinking, reasoning, and feeling. Children were held to adult standards both at home and in the world of work.

Over the past one hundred years, we have gradually rejected these assumptions and adopted an alternate perspective: Childhood is its own unique stage of life. Adults and children do not think or reason in the same way. Children are not small-sized adults.

Beginning in the mid-nineteenth century, legislators enacted laws prohibiting child labor and creating a protected zone called "childhood." Around the same time, Victorian society began insulating children from adulthood's violence and sexuality.

The Bible's authors often reflect a developmental understanding of childhood. Children do not think and reason as adults. "When I was a child, I spoke like a child, I thought like a child," Paul writes the Corinthians. "When I became an adult, I put an end to childish ways" (1 Corinthians 13:11). Luke's gospel reminds readers that Jesus grew in understanding and wisdom as he grew physically. "And Jesus increased in wisdom and in years" (Luke 2:52).

Just as the human body develops and grows, the human mind evolves and changes. This insight has important implications for Christian teaching and faith formation. Keeping in touch with teaching means keeping in touch with theories of cognitive or mental development and their implications for Christian faith formation.

A Simple Conclusion That Only a Genius Could Think Of

No one has contributed more to our contemporary practice of graded curricular resources than Jean Piaget. Piaget was born in Switzerland in 1896. At age ten, he discovered an albino sparrow and wrote a brief article about it, which was published. As a result, the curator of the local natural history museum asked Piaget to become his assistant. Working at the museum, Piaget developed a lifelong interest in how living things evolve and change. This interest laid the foundation for Piaget's theories of mental development and change.

In his early twenties, Piaget moved to Paris and began working for a colleague of Alfred Binet, who had created the first intelligence tests. Piaget's task was to conduct experiments that could help standardize early psychological testing. Asking children a question, he recorded at what age most children were able to answer it correctly. Using their answers, he set performance norms that were age-appropriate for children.

Piaget, however, modified his task. He did not simply record whether children could answer correctly or not. He also interviewed them to uncover their reasoning. In the process of his research, Piaget made the discovery for which he is most famous: Children at different ages give different answers and use fundamentally different reasoning and logic. Children at different ages do not possess the same conception of the world around them.

Younger children are not dumber than older children or adults. They simply think differently than their older counterparts.

At age twenty-five, Piaget's research made him world-famous. By age forty, he had earned an honorary doctorate from Harvard and his name was known by educators around the globe. Piaget's conclusions, as Albert Einstein put it, were so simple that only a genius could have discovered them.

The new science of the brain has confirmed many of Piaget's basic insights. Piaget studied children using only observation and interviews. With today's sophisticated equipment, contemporary researchers can actually look inside the developing brain's structure and chemistry. As a result, neuroscience is enriching, expanding, and explaining what Piaget first described more than seventy-five years ago.

Piaget's insights altered forever how church educators and leaders thought about Christian teaching and faith formation. Keeping in touch with teaching means keeping in touch with Piaget and his successors. In many ways, our current practice of graded curriculum owes its origins to Piaget's insights and observations.

Stages of Cognitive Development

Piaget identified four stages of cognitive development from birth to adolescence [see Figure 3.1].[1]

Sensorimotor (Birth to Age 2). From birth until about age two, infants know the world only through their physical interactions with it. They lack internal mental structures to transform sense perceptions into thoughts. They solve problems by physical movement rather than by thinking. They taste, touch, roll, or push in order to learn about their world. These early sensory experiences lay the foundation for all later mental processes.

Recent brain research underscores the sensorimotor stage's importance in human development. Most of our brain's physical growth occurs in the first year of life. The growing infant is producing neurons and laying down neural pathways at a tremendous rate. Just as a gardener creates a lawn's hardscape—its basic structures and pathways—before the first bulb or shrub is planted, so our brain's hardscape—its basic neural patterning and structure—is created before the first mental operation has begun. Some of these pathways will later be pruned away if they are not used. But the richness or poverty of the brain's early hardscape inevitably shapes how we may love, know, and serve God later in life.

Christian educators are rightly concerned with the sensorimotor experiences of infants and toddlers. During these years, the brain is structuring itself and laying down basic neural patterns. We learn and make meaning across the lifespan by means of these pathways. Our early neural hardscape determines whether we will be capable of wonder and imagination, critical and creative thought, commitment and compassion. A mature faith has its origin in this early neural hardscape.

Sensorimotor children require extensive adult support and interaction. These interactions provide them with vital sensory stimulation: music; art; touch; play; or dance. Churches

Figure 3.1: Piaget's Stages of Cognitive Development

Name	Age	Characteristics	Implications
Sensorimotor	Birth–Age 2	Knows the world through physical interaction No internal mental operations, only sensory experiences Creation of neural pathways and patterning	Provide the growing child lots of verbal and sensory interaction with adults.
Preoperational	Ages 2–7	Acquisition of language and ability to use symbols Can overfocus on unimportant details Unable to "walk in someone else's shoes" Weak sense of cause-and-effect relationships Concrete, literal thinking	Support parallel play rather than force team games or group games. Check to see how children are appropriating or understanding the lesson. (Do they have the main point or a peripheral detail?) Arrange multiple points of interest. Carefully distinguish between magical thinking and religious faith. Teach through relationships of love and care.
Concrete Operational	Ages 7-11	Strong emphasis on fairness Sharp distinction between real and "pretend" Cannot think hypothetically or poetically	Ensure that a healthy understanding of real and pretend can emerge around key biblical ideas and beliefs. Find opportunities for moral and ethical instruction and commitment.
Formal Operational	Age 11 and Older	Can think about how they are thinking Capable of taking alternative perspectives Can envision and commit to high ideals	Provide preaching and learning based on abstract themes and doctrines. Explore opportunities for making faith commitments. Harness high ideals for purposes of vocation and ministry.

honor the needs of sensorimotor children when they treat their nursery programs as more than babysitting services for parents.

Living Hope's leadership believes the most important thing their church can do to foster adult faith formation is to encourage art and music in young children. The congregation sponsors an afterschool art class for community children. It holds a summer music camp using its own facilities and members. It hosts an annual religion and the arts festival where music, weaving, sculpture, and paintings are displayed and judged. When the public schools eliminated music programs due to budget cuts, Living Hope began offering afterschool music lessons. The congregation sees these activities as part of its long-term evangelization effort. If the church wants adult Christians capable of mature faith, then it must begin laying a foundation for imagination and wonder early in life.

Art and music create the neural pathways that adults need to encounter the mystery and awe, the wonder and majesty of God. Early exposure to art and music hardwires the brain with imaginative and creative capacities needed to love, know, and serve God with the whole heart, soul, strength, and mind.

Crossways Church recently restructured its nursery ministry. The first challenge was to transfer nursery oversight from the evangelism committee to the education committee. Crossways' leadership had begun a nursery ministry primarily to attract younger families who wanted a safe, clean place for their children while they were in worship or Sunday school. The nursery's stated purpose was to attract new families, not to lay a foundation for Christian faith formation. Crossways now wanted to signal that its nursery was an educational ministry. It was where the foundation for later Christian education was established.

Crossways had staffed its nursery with teenage volunteers. They discovered, however, that most of these volunteers were not interacting with children. They were watching passively while children played with toys, crawled about the room, or napped. The education committee recruited and trained new volunteers with different expectations. The new volunteers were older and they were expected to have a much higher level of involvement with infants and toddlers. The committee supported these higher expectations through initial and ongoing training as well as appropriate nursery resources.

To evaluate its nursery resources, the education committee decided to conduct an inventory of nursery supplies, toys, and curriculum. Crossways Church had previously stocked its nursery with hand-me-down toys donated by families whose own children had outgrown them. They were both dated and worn. The committee discarded these toys and made a fresh start. A local artist painted biblical characters on the walls. They hung brightly colored, bird-shaped kites from the ceiling. Using catalogs that specialized in early childhood resources, they purchased new furnishings that provided mental stimulation and active engagement.

The nursery at Crossways is more than a babysitting service. It directly contributes to Christian teaching and faith formation. It builds the foundation for what will later happen in Crossways's ministries with children, youth, and adults. The leadership of Crossways knows that early childhood experiences shape an adult capacity for spiritual experience.

Preoperational (Ages 2-7). During the preoperational stage, children acquire the ability to use symbols and language. Children can represent objects internally as mental images. They no longer need an actual physical ball to think about playing with a ball. They can think about a car without needing physically to hold a toy car or look at a picture of a car. They can represent an object mentally without its actual physical presence.

Preoperational children do not perceive complex situations. They see only one aspect or quality at a time. In problem solving, preoperational children therefore cannot see the connections between various parts of a problem. They overfocus on one detail. In a Sunday school lesson, they may treat a small, peripheral fact as the main point.

Trang's teacher had just read the story of Jesus' birth. "Why was Jesus born in a manger?" her teacher asked. "Because of the star," Trang replied. Her teacher was puzzled. "No, Trang, that's not correct," Ms. Liu said. "Does anyone else know?" Trang's shoulders dropped and she looked at her feet. *What was wrong with my answer?* she wondered.

Trang was responding as any preoperational child might. She had focused on a particular detail in the story. Trang's answer made perfect sense to her. Unfortunately Ms. Liu was following the script in her Sunday school lesson. She consequently did not take time to explore why Trang thought the star explained Jesus' birth in a manger. If she had understood the preoperational child's tendency to overfocus on details, Ms. Liu might have asked follow-up questions to draw out Trang's logic and guide her toward another response. She might have entered sympathetically into Trang's preoperational logic and reasoning, helping her clarify and grow in her faith. Rather than deflate Trang, such an approach might have opened her to further learning.

Preoperational children are self-centered or egocentric. They are at the center of their world. They believe everyone sees, thinks, and experiences exactly as they do. Preoperational children are not able to place themselves in another's shoes even for a short time.

They thus tend to engage in parallel play. They play alongside each other without genuinely interacting or sharing. Each child lives in his or her own egocentric world. Classrooms and activities for preoperational children require plenty of room and multiple points of interest that each child can individually pursue. Group exercises and cooperative learning are typically not effective with preoperational children.

These needs have obvious implications for Sunday school classrooms. Preoperational children need large rooms where they can engage in parallel play and explore widely their environment. Teachers need space to create multiple learning centers. Such configurations are sometimes difficult in older buildings with small classrooms originally designed for an era when even small children sat quietly and listened to teachers read a Sunday school lesson to them. Even in these situations, however, Christian educators can explore creative and innovative solutions that provide adequate space for preoperational children.

The egocentricity of preoperational children also means that rules are fluid and may be turned to selfish ends. Anyone who has intervened in a game where preschoolers are fighting because "Aaron keeps changing the rules" knows this characteristic and its effect on classroom activities. Preoperational children have difficulty understanding the concept of rigid rules. Ethical or moral reasoning is limited to their own perspective.

Finally, preoperational children have a poor understanding of cause and effect. They observe static states and ignore the transformations that occur between them. The absence of cause-and-effect thinking means preoperational children are especially prone to magical thinking. Once magical thinking is firmly entrenched in a preoperational child's religious education, it can sow the seeds for a later crisis of faith. Many adults experience a loss of faith when their magical trust in prayer is disappointed because a loved one dies or suffers in spite of their fervent prayers.

Preoperational children acquire their faith primarily through the love and care they experience from adults. The quality of Sunday school teachers' care and the genuineness of their faith are far more important for faith formation than factual information or theological concepts. Relationships, not information, are critical for preoperational children.

Concrete Operational (Ages 7-11). The concrete operational stage roughly parallels a child's elementary school years. These children can employ internal concepts to think about objects or events in the world. They can use mathematical concepts, tell time, and write.

Elementary-age children think concretely. They focus on people and objects that are present, visible, and accessible. They cannot easily imagine hypothetical situations. Because they focus on what is rather than what could be, they take stories and concepts literally. These children are usually incapable of metaphorical or poetic thinking. A sharp distinction exists between pretend and real.

Children at this stage also take rules and norms seriously. Having lost the previous stage's egocentricity, they understand the concept of shared norms and hold both themselves and others to agreed-upon standards. They are committed to "playing by the rules." As a result, fairness and a clear sense of right and wrong usually characterize these years. Sunday school leaders often emphasize moral instruction and biblical themes such as the Ten Commandments with this age group because these children so easily understand moral rules and ethical norms.

Because concrete operational children focus on names, dates, places, and other tangible information, Sunday schools usually emphasize memory work during these years. They may even establish reward systems for memorizing the books of the Bible, the Lord's Prayer, the Apostles' Creed, or other catechetical material.

Roleplay, simulations, games, crafts, and other hands-on activities capitalize on this age's concrete operational style. Many congregations begin to involve children in choirs, service groups, and midweek programs during these years. Now that these children have moved beyond the preoperational stage's egocentricity, group activities naturally appeal to them.

On the other hand, these years are not without their pitfalls. Some religious educators have expressed concern that Sunday schools unintentionally inoculate children against religious faith during these years. Children often have difficulty grasping the sometimes metaphorical nature of Christian symbols, stories, and doctrines because they make such sharp distinctions between real and pretend. If the psalms describe God as sitting on a throne in heaven and hurling thunder and lightning upon the earth, then God is quite literally an older, bearded man on a throne. Extremely concrete, literal concepts of God can develop during this stage.

These concepts may later become a stumbling block for faith as adults face life's tragedies, crises, and moral ambiguities. Some adults decide the concrete notions of Christian faith formed during this period are at worst false and at best irrelevant. Abandoning these concepts, they have nothing else with which to replace them. The church's religious education can thus inadvertently create adult agnostics and atheists.

Formal Operational (Age 11 and Above). During these years, thought takes wing. Adolescents can now think abstractly and metaphorically. They are not limited to concrete, literal thinking but can "think about how they are thinking." They can examine both their thoughts and the assumptions behind their thoughts. Formal operations make poetry and metaphor, imagination and creativity possible. Music, art, poetry, and metaphor become important teaching tools during these years.

As with previous cognitive stages, changes in the brain's chemical and physical structure influence when formal operations become possible. As we noted in the previous chapter, myelin helps our neural pathways fire more rapidly. Myelin begins coating our neurons at birth and is released in stages. It begins in the lower brain and eventually spreads to the prefrontal cortex, where our higher-order thinking resides. This may explain why Piaget observed that higher-order thinking appears only in adolescence, since myelin does not coat our prefrontal cortex until then.

Adolescents capable of formal operations can create ideals for themselves. They are no longer just carried by the flow of life. They can reflect on people, events, and relationships. This capacity to envision high ideals means that adolescents become highly critical when adults and adult institutions fail to live up to stated ideals or purposes. Christian teaching and learning now focus on how to harness these high ideals and their energy for gospel purposes.

At this stage, adolescents are able to think about abstract Christian doctrines of God, salvation, and sin. They can understand the symbols and metaphors central to Christian faith. Confirmation, baptism, or reaffirmation of one's baptismal covenant consequently occur during these years.

Adult Stages of Cognitive Development. Piaget believed that everyone moved from concrete operations to formal operations by around age twelve. More recent research suggests that this capacity for abstract thought and poetic thinking develops more slowly in some people. Indeed, many adults never move beyond the level of concrete operations. Some researchers propose that no more than half of all adults in Western societies reach the level of formal operations. The other half either does not attain or does not employ formal operations.[2]

WAYS WE COME TO KNOW OUR WORLD

Piaget's primary interest was explaining how people come to know their world. He was interested in how we grow and learn. His stages of cognitive development chronicle how we learn to interpret our experience as we grow and mature.

Piaget's developmental stages provide Christian educators with important clues about effective instructional strategies for different age groups. If Sunday school teachers know that preoperational children tend to overfocus on details and thus miss a story's main point, they can better design classroom activities to ensure that students grasp the essential biblical message. Keeping in touch with teaching means keeping in touch with teaching strategies based on Piaget's observations.

We Live by Learning

Learning is a uniquely human attribute. Reptiles are born with automatic responses. Mammals come into the world with emotions and instincts that guide their behavior. But human beings must learn in order to survive. We live by learning. Our family dog, Wesley, does not need to learn. He operates by instinct. Wesley can be trained, but he does not learn. My sons, on the other hand, survive by learning, not by instinct. Since birth, Robert and Jonathan have continually organized and reorganized their experiences as they adapt to constantly changing circumstances.

Learning as a Dance of Mind and Muscle. Our learning does not occur in a vacuum, however. We are more than disembodied mental will-o-the-wisps. As the science of the brain suggests, learning is a physical, bodily experience as well as a mental phenomenon. This was also Piaget's insight into how we think and learn. We learn with our bodies as well as with our brains. Interaction between the growing body and the constantly active mind propels cognitive development forward.

Learning always involves this complex dance between physical and mental development, according to Piaget. His developmental stages sketch the dance steps by which children make sense of their changing world as brain and body grow. Expanding physical powers create novel experiences, which children organize into new patterns of meaning. These new mental patterns then allow children to envision still more complex bodily and social experiences, which stimulate the next stage of mental growth.

The day Robert and Jonathan learned to walk, their worlds grew larger. Their worlds took another quantum leap forward when they mastered riding a bicycle. Physical changes expanded their mental and social worlds. They could go farther and create more complex experiences for themselves. These new experiences, in turn, triggered yet further restructuring of their mental operations.

We live by learning, by making sense of our bodily and social experience. Both brain and muscle contribute to this process. Since brain and muscle develop physically as we grow, our knowing changes as we mature. Learning, then, is at its origins a physical activity. It begins in the infant's grasping and seeing. It matures into the child riding the bicycle or throwing a basketball. It is also a social experience. Learning always requires other people. A child alone in the wilderness, raised by wolves, does not develop into a fully human person. We make meaning in community with others.

At first, this community is the small world of the infant's family. Later, it expands to include other people and institutions. Over time, we acquire the shared meanings common to our culture or society. Our physical, social, and mental development intersect and mutually influence one another. Physical and mental growth allow us to inhabit a larger social world. Experiences in this larger social world stretch us to meet new physical and mental challenges.

Mental Maps and Learning

Through these evolving social, mental, and physical experiences, we develop fixed ideas about how things work and what has significance. These fixed ideas serve as road maps by which we navigate our way through life. We sometimes call these fixed ideas "mental maps" because they function like road maps. Piaget called them schemes. Others call them schemas, mental models, assumptive frameworks, or meaning-perspectives. Whatever we call them, they function like road maps because they help us know where we are and where we are going in life.

Learning Begins in Wonder, Not Need. Learning begins when we wonder what some new experience means. The new experience may be physical or social or even mental. Our answer transforms raw experience into a deposit of remembered meaning. As other experiences occur, they are connected or contrasted to these deposits of remembered meaning. Over time, these remembered deposits become patterns of meaning that guide our thinking and acting.

These mental maps are always changing. A friend recently told me about his winter vacation to Florida. Not having been to Florida before, he had consulted his father about the best routes to travel. Reaching into his desk, his father pulled out a map of the southeastern United States. Giving the map to his son, he showed him the best route to follow—the route that he himself always used. My friend did not look closely at the map but tucked it into his bags when he packed.

As he and his family made their way southward, his wife began to question why they were traveling on roads that took them directly through large cities and small towns. They could make faster time if they went on the interstate highways, she insisted. "But the map doesn't show interstate highways in this part of Florida," my friend replied. His wife looked more closely at the map. It had been printed in 1966.

We would never think of taking a road trip with an out-of-date map. Highway maps change to reflect new roads, bridges, or bypasses. In the same way, our mental maps change to reflect new experiences. As we move from one of Piaget's stages to the next, we alter our maps.

We use three skills to alter our mental maps: generalization, selection, and interpretation. We generalize when we see recurrent patterns or repeating experiences and create a picture of how the world works from them. We are selective in our experiencing of the world. We do not record sense experiences like a camera records impressions of light and color. We notice some things and ignore others. Some cultures notice fine distinctions between different kinds of snow. One culture may base its language on tonal qualities that another culture cannot hear. We are always selecting from our sensory experience which details we will observe. Finally, we use interpretation to make sense of experience. We see connections. We draw conclusions. We bring things together into meaningful patterns.

These three skills allow us to construct and reconstruct our mental maps. This process begins at birth and continues throughout our lives. After many sleepless nights with newborns, I am convinced that children do not naturally fall asleep—at least not on their parents' timetable. They must learn to fall asleep. As a puppy, our family dog made a few tight circles around his pillow, curled up, and went to sleep. Robert and Jonathan, on the other hand, lacked this instinct for falling asleep. They had to learn this behavior.

Robert and Jonathan's tired parents engaged in all kinds of complex teaching to help them learn how to fall asleep. We created a predictable routine—a bedtime ritual—that eased them into sleep. We provided positive reinforcement for falling asleep and negative reinforcement for staying awake. Robert and Jonathan gradually transformed these bedtime experiences into a pattern of meaning, a mental map, that said: "It's time to fall asleep and this is how to do it." They used generalization, selection, and interpretation. Their learning was both a physical activity happening in their bodies and a social activity that involved interacting with other people—in this case, their sleep-deprived parents.

Process and Data Maps. Mental maps are packets in which the brain organizes and stores information. Data maps organize facts and information. Process maps organize procedures and sequences. A data map contains knowledge *about* something. A process map contains knowledge *about how to do* something.

Some process maps operate like scripts or sequenced actions. My sons have a process map for Sunday school. They know that when we arrive, they go to the fellowship hall where all the children and youth assemble for an opening exercise. Then they go to their classroom. When they enter the room, they continue following this same process map. They expect certain things to happen in a predictable order. When a substitute teacher does not know this process map and scrambles the script, they come home complaining about the teacher.

Sunday school teachers almost unconsciously help students master all kinds of data and process maps. When children learn the books of the Bible, they are mastering a data map. When they are taught to find a particular Bible verse or passage, they are learning a process map.

Positive Contributions of Mental Maps. The mental maps we develop through generalization, selection, and interpretation are the source of both our best and worst qualities. They are where our values and beliefs dwell. They also support our biases and stereotypes [see Figure 3.2].

Figure 3.2: Effects of Mental Maps or Schemas

Positive	Negative
Establish expectations, including what to pay attention to	Result in selective perception
Organize information so we can understand large amounts of information quickly	Cause overgeneralization
	Cause us to jump to conclusions
Make learning and comprehension possible	Result in "mind reading"—attributing motives or thoughts to others
Guide action	Cause us to exaggerate—something trivial is given too much significance because it fits a pattern we have
Relate new information to what we already know	

Mental maps make a positive contribution to Christian teaching and learning. Indeed they are pivotal for learning.

First, they direct our attention. As certain patterns are strengthened, we recognize them more quickly. They also allow us to understand large amounts of information quickly. They enable the brain to connect lots of information in interlocking networks.

Second, they allow us to store and retrieve new knowledge more quickly. Spider webs of meaning allow the brain to have multiple neural pathways for recalling a particular piece of information. These neural nets are infinitely expandable. Everything can be connected to everything else through some data chain. We think in wholes, not parts, because that is how the mind is organized. The brain simultaneously perceives and creates both parts and wholes.

Christian educators too often focus on a "bottom-up" teaching that begins with parts rather than wholes. They assume Christian belief and practice can be broken down into small parts—facts, verses, doctrines. Each can be taught individually and students will somehow combine them on their own into meaningful wholes. But children and even adults do not always assemble these parts in the way that educators assume they will. As a result, many Christians have a fragmented, incoherent, and partial understanding of Christian faith.

Discoveries about how mental maps work are now leading educators in the opposite direction. The brain learns and thinks in wholes, not parts. It operates by a "top-down" strategy that begins with the whole map into which individual parts can be fitted. If we lack the big picture, we may not know where an isolated piece of information fits. Or worse, we may misconstrue how it fits into the larger picture and misuse or misunderstand what we have learned.

Third, mental maps make learning and comprehension possible. If I say, "The seams were split so the notes were sour" you may have no idea what I mean unless you already have a mental map for bagpipes.

Fourth, mental maps guide our actions. Once we have a mental map of a particular activity, we no longer have to devote mental energy to performing that action or behavior. Our energy and mental focus can instead go toward more complex or novel experiences. When I am driving my car, I do not think about what to do when the light turns green. I respond automatically by putting my foot on the gas pedal and going forward. I am not thinking, "Now, what does it mean when the light turns green? What shall I do next?" A well-established mental model guides my action.

Finally, mental maps help us remember and learn because we associate new information with existing patterns. New information is massaged into what we already know. Once we understand the concept of New Testament and Old Testament, we can fit lots of events and people into a coherent historical time line. Without this schema, we are confronted with a confusing jumble of names, books, and events.

Defending Against Schema Attacks. Mental maps or schemas also have negative consequences. All schemas involve selective perception. At its best, selective attention allows us to focus on what is most important. At its worst, we see information in only one way and discount all other possibilities. Alternative stimuli are edited out and ignored. Our mental maps cause us to overgeneralize.

Schemas cause us to jump to conclusions. They make us believe we can read someone's mind and know what that person "really means." The brain thinks it recognizes a pattern and fills in the missing data. It hears a particular word or phrase and completes the sentence. But we may have misunderstood completely what someone was saying to us. When this happens, we have suffered a schema attack.

Walk into any church and you will find people experiencing schema attacks. They happen in the Sunday school classroom as an argument breaks out over whose biblical interpretation is more faithful. They occur in the education committee as members struggle to reach a decision but talk past each other. Schema attacks happen in youth groups. Mariel ignores her youth fellowship's guest speaker immediately after she hears the word "temptation." She has heard her parents' lectures on sin and temptation. She does not need to listen to them again. Unfortunately, this schema attack means that Mariel misses an important learning opportunity.

Mental maps or schemas have important implications for Christian teaching and faith formation. The first step is to become aware of how these schemas guide our thinking and deciding. Once we are aware of how we think and learn by means of these mental maps, we are better able to monitor ourselves for a schema attack. We are able to think about how we are thinking.

Once Sunday school teachers understand how students form and transform their mental maps, they can design classroom activities that enhance the brain's ability to learn. They can help students more easily learn and remember Christian teachings. They can design instruction that more powerfully forms faith in children, youth, and adults.

WAYS WE ADAPT OUR MENTAL MAPS

Church educators help Christians internalize mental maps that deepen their love, knowledge, and service to God and neighbor. Piaget identified two ways we adapt our mental maps to new information. The first he called accommodation; the second, assimilation. Both have important implications for how church educators approach their task.

Assimilation describes the addition of more information or facts to existing mental maps. Accommodation involves the creation or restructuring of our mental maps. We accommodate our thinking to new experiences. We construct new roadmaps or mental models to guide our thinking and acting. Accommodation generally occurs less often than assimilation and is usually more difficult. To better understand how accommodation and assimilation work, consider this example from everyday life:

A group of Sunday school teachers has gone to a weekend conference in an unfamiliar city. They decide to eat at a well-known restaurant in a nearby suburb. They ask the conference host for directions. Setting out in their car, they closely follow the instructions and arrive for lunch. Had they encountered a construction detour, however, they would have been quite lost. Even with their directions, they had to concentrate carefully on their map and look intently for street signs.

At the end of the conference, they decide to visit the same restaurant. This time, they hardly pay attention to the street signs and map. They navigate to the restaurant with minimal difficulty. In fact, they are talking and laughing most of the way. As they go, they even stop to shop at some stores they looked up in the telephone book.

These teachers were engaged in both accommodation and assimilation. When they were learning a new way to the restaurant, these Sunday school teachers concentrated on what they were doing. They were unsure how many blocks to go, whether to turn left or right, or if they had gone too far. Later they knew the path well enough to begin filling in details and noticing other things along the route.

Accommodation is like learning a new route to the restaurant. We are accommodating what we know to new conditions and circumstances. We go slowly and pay a great deal of attention as we develop this new mental map. We may even be confused or puzzled along the way. We are not sure this new mental map is really accurate or will take us where we want to go.

Once the teachers had this new map firmly in place, they could engage in assimilation. They added new detail to something they already knew. Once we have a map firmly in place, we can easily assimilate new information to it. We notice additional facts and details, including them in this existing mental map.

Brian's Sunday school teachers have always taught him that if you go to church every week, God will not let bad things happen to you. But Brian's older brother has just been killed in an automobile accident. Brian's present experience is challenging his previous schema or understanding of God. With the help of a sensitive pastor, Brian's mental map of how God works is fundamentally restructured. After much grief and anger, Brian comes through this experience with a richer, deeper understanding of God and himself. Accommodation has occurred.

Accommodation generally occurs less often than assimilation. Accommodation is more difficult because learning is seldom free from emotions. We have beliefs, values, and attitudes attached to our knowledge, to our mental maps. These beliefs, values, and attitudes carry emotional power. They create resistance to learning new mental maps or acquiring new mental models.

When Christian educators introduce new concepts or ideas into adult classes, they often encounter resistance. New ideas or interpretations may challenge deeply held beliefs and powerful values. Participants come expecting assimilative learning. They anticipate that they will add more detail to their existing mental maps. They hope to acquire more facts or arguments that bolster their current convictions. They expect assimilation and consequently resist accommodation. They downshift into their R-brains, which trust only precedent, habit, and predictable routine.

EFFECTIVE TEACHING FOCUSES ON HOW WE KNOW, NOT JUST WHAT WE KNOW

Faithful and effective Christian educators focus not just on what students know but also on how they know it. They foster both assimilation and accommodation.

Moving Beyond the Public School Model of Teaching. Borrowing from the public school model, Sunday school teachers have assessed what students know in order to determine where to begin instruction or whether their teaching has been successful. For the most part, they have not tried to assess students' mental maps—how prior Christian knowledge is organized and held.

They have also assumed that the way to transform students' knowing is to provide them with more information or new facts. But rather than change people's thinking, these facts may simply be assimilated into how they already understand Christian faith.

The public school model has focused on sequencing individual parts rather than teaching the whole picture. Selecting the proper media or drill and practice have been more important than helping students think about how they think.

Sunday schools have often adopted these same practices. Memory work focuses on parts. Teachers assume that students are able to see the connections between individual Bible verses and the larger themes of Christian life. Yet people may not grasp the connections or see overarching biblical themes such as mercy, hospitality, forgiveness, or shalom as peace with justice.

Sunday school teachers may use videotapes or other media to tell biblical stories. Yet they sometimes do little actual processing of what students are thinking or learning as they watch these media. They assume students will make the proper connections and create the appropriate meaning from what they are seeing and hearing. But this is not necessarily what happens. Children may be learning something quite different from what teachers intend. The problem is not the video. It is the failure to process actively with learners what meaning they have made from what they have just watched.

Through the lens of Piaget's modes of learning, church educators begin to see other possibilities. Their emphasis shifts from teaching what biblically knowledgeable Christians should know to helping children and youth understand how they are knowing Christian faith and practice.

How We Know Determines *What* We Know. I was once asked to consult with a congregation struggling to embrace its changing community. This formerly small-town church found itself in the midst of a growing suburb. The congregation was not growing, however. In fact, it was in sharp decline. Church leaders felt the key challenge was offering hospitality. Long-term members felt threatened by newcomers so they were not welcoming. I was therefore asked to lead some workshops on hospitality that might enable church leaders to embrace a new, more welcoming vision.

I decided to use the Emmaus Road story in Luke 24. After a brief overview and introduction, I asked participants to work in small groups. They were to describe how the two disciples responded to the stranger on the road. I then planned to ask them to compare these responses with how they responded to Sunday visitors. It seemed like a simple, foolproof plan. Unfortunately, their responses completely derailed my plan. Their analysis of the Emmaus Road story went in an entirely different direction than I had envisioned.

"Well," one group began. "The two disciples told the stranger what the rules were and how things were done. Then they invited him to join them."

"This is just like our church," another group reported. "We invite people, but it's really a waste of time because after a few Sundays they disappear the way Jesus does in this story. They never come back."

These teachers had definite mental maps, and they were assimilating the Emmaus Road story into their maps rather than allowing the biblical narrative to restructure their thinking. What the teachers knew was not the issue. How they knew it—the mental map into which they fitted new facts and information—was the problem. Too often we focus only on what students are learning. But if we ignore how they know it, learners may reach conclusions dramatically at odds with what we believe we are teaching.

Furthermore, focusing on how students know new information allows Christian educators to be more intentional in the teaching strategies they adopt. Some teaching strategies best contribute to assimilation. Others better foster restructuring or accommodation. Since not all strategies are appropriate for all types of learning, Christian educators need to choose the instructional strategies most appropriate for their content and goals.

Our next chapter will explore some practical implications of mental maps and how they evolve and change. We will also describe concrete teaching strategies that help Christian educators focus not just on what students know but on how they know it.

Deepening Your Learning

1. Take a field trip to your church's infant/toddler nursery. Sit on the floor or lie down. Observe what you see. Apply what you know about Piaget's theory. What do children learn in this space? How could you help your congregation make it a more effective educational ministry?

2. One implication of Piaget's concrete operational stage is that we sometimes develop literal, concrete Christian beliefs. Later in life, these concrete understandings can cause a crisis of faith. Can you remember experiencing such a crisis of faith? Who or what helped you restructure some of your mental maps?

3. Describe a schema attack you recently experienced. What can you learn about this experience that helps you become a better Christian educator or church leader?

4. Design a Sunday school, Bible class, or youth group lesson in which you approach the topic in a "bottom-up" manner—starting with parts and building toward the big picture. Now design a lesson on the same topic using a "top-down" approach that starts with the big picture and fills in the parts. What do you notice about these two designs? How do they affect you as the teacher? How do you think learners would respond to each design? Why?

Endnotes

1 See *Learning and Instruction,* by Richard Hamilton and Elizabeth Ghatala (McGraw-Hill, 1994), pages 206-251.

2 See *Learning in Adulthood: A Comprehensive Guide,* by Sharan B. Merriam and Rosemary S. Caffarella (Jossey-Bass, 1991), page 183.

CHAPTER FOUR

Set These Words Upon Your Heart

Cognitive Strategies for Teaching

Teaching is a two-pronged undertaking. On the one hand, it is a subversive activity. Good teaching causes people to pause and reflect. It alters perceptions and changes lives. It leaves learners different people than they were before. Teaching is also a conserving enterprise. It passes on the hard-won wisdom of earlier generations. It transmits the distilled insights of those who have gone before us. It reminds us of those things that make for meaningful and abundant life.

The Christian faith is a teaching faith. It includes both transmission and transformation, assimilation and accommodation. "Keep these words that I am commanding you today in your heart," Moses instructs the Israelites; "Recite them to your children and talk about them when you are at home and when you are away, when you lie down and when you rise. Bind them as a sign on your hand, fix them as an emblem on your forehead, and write them on the doorposts of your house and on your gates" (Deuteronomy 6:6-9). For the author of Deuteronomy, we cannot perform what we do not know. If Israel is to keep God's covenant, then the people must learn God's statutes and commandments.

Matthew's gospel, in particular, emphasizes the church's teaching ministry. The church's central task is transmission and transformation. The risen Christ commands his disciples: "Go therefore and make disciples [that is, "learners"] of all nations, baptizing them in the name of the Father and of the Son and of the Holy Spirit, and teaching them to obey everything that I have commanded you" (Matthew 28:19-20). Matthew places great emphasis upon teaching because he expects Christians to do what they are taught: practice justice and mercy so God's reign may be embodied in the world. Transmission and transformation are still central to the church's teaching ministry.

Piaget's insights provide fertile ground for practical teaching strategies that transmit the good news of Jesus Christ and transform human lives. These strategies are particularly important in an era when many complain of church members' biblical illiteracy. People cannot use in daily life what they do not recall or remember. They cannot embody what they have not learned. Faithful Christian witness depends on a rich Christian memory that informs everyday thinking and deciding. Cognitive teaching strategies represent ways Christian educators can strengthen the muscle of Christian memory in learners.

THREE TYPES OF COGNITIVE STRATEGIES

Cognitive strategies derived from Piaget's work can be divided into three basic categories: chunking strategies, spatial strategies, and bridging strategies.[1] Some specific examples of these strategies contribute primarily to assimilation. Others foster accommodative learning. A few assist with both assimilation and accommodation.

Figure 4.1: Types of Cognitive Strategies

Spatial ← Teaching Strategies → Bridging

——— = a subcomponent of

Chunking

Effective Teaching Helps Learners See the Big Picture. Most of these strategies—particularly chunking and spatial strategies—actually mimic how the brain processes and stores information. In processing, storing, and retrieving information, the brain operates by association and interconnection.

For this reason, although the analogy between a computer and the human brain is common in our everyday speech, it is not at all helpful—especially to Christian educators [see Figure 4.2].

The computer on which I am typing randomly stores information in available space. The human brain is a vast neural net, a spider web of interconnected experiences, memories, and facts. Nothing is randomly stored. We cannot "defrag" our brains the way we do our computers. We think by means of relationships and connections, not randomly stored bytes of data.

Figure 4.2: Contrasts Between the Brain and a Computer

Computer	Human Brain
Data can be entered randomly and retrieved.	We learn better when material is organized and connected.
Data is accessible forever.	Memories can fade over time.
Each piece of data is stored separately and randomly.	Memory is a network of interconnected information.
We have to have the address or file name to access data.	We can access our memories of facts, events, and people in many ways—all of which can fail.
Retrieval of data has no effect on the data itself or its accessibility.	Remembering something can both change the memory and enhance our ability to retrieve it again.
Data must be intentionally entered.	We are always learning whether we intend to or not.

This weblike quality of memory has enormous implications for Christian education. We learn by relationship and association. Our brains do not effectively process information when they perceive it as random facts and bytes of data. We need the big picture. Then we know how the parts fit. You can input random bits of information into a computer and it will sort them into categories. But our brains do not work that way.

The randomness of many children's participation in Christian education means that they often fail to grasp the big picture even when they can recite the memory verses. If we were feeding data into a computer, such random bytes of data would be acceptable. But this approach does not work with the human brain.

Sunday school teachers often assume that once children have learned a particular parable or Bible story, it remains accessible forever. That may be true in a computer. Once a file is created, the data is always there. But human memory is not like a computer. Memories can fade over time. Faith formation involves helping students revisit stories and events from fresh perspectives so that new connections are made and memories are strengthened.

Piaget and the new science of the brain suggest ways that Christian educators can help learners to create these neural nets of knowing and remembering. These neural nets are absolutely crucial because we cannot use what we do not know. We cannot embody the good news of God's reign if we do not know what Scripture and tradition tell us about it.

Cognitive strategies not only organize and connect knowledge, they supply us with multiple points and pathways through which we can access or retrieve it. They focus not just on what we are learning but also on how we are learning it.

Chunking Strategies

When Robert and Jonathan were little, their mother and I would often give them chores that required sorting skills: Separate the forks from the spoons and put them in the drawer. Sort the towels from the washcloths and stack them in different piles. Sorting or categorizing is a basic mental function. We naturally sort, categorize, and classify everything. Piaget's research examined how children sorted and categorized objects at different ages and stages.

Chunking strategies build on this natural tendency to "chunk," or categorize, things. These strategies allow us to handle large amounts of information quickly. When we chunk information into large categories, we learn and remember material more efficiently. We can also create smaller chunks within larger ones, allowing us to remember still larger amounts of information.

For example, we chunk the Bible into "Old Testament" and "New Testament." Then, within these large chunks, we create smaller chunks such as "Law," "History," "Prophecy," and "Wisdom" or "Gospels," "History," and "Letters." If we did not chunk or categorize in this way, it would be difficult to remember where to find a particular book of the Bible.

Good teachers almost naturally use chunking strategies. With minimal effort and an understanding of mental maps or schemas, they help their students learn and recall large amounts of biblical or doctrinal knowledge.

Chunking strategies can be used with either assimilation or accommodation. Teaching children to chunk knowledge into easily remembered categories may help them create new mental maps. It may also allow learners to add more detail to what they already know.

Chunking and the Process of Human Memory. Chunking strategies are important because they closely reflect how memory itself is organized. The standard model of human memory consists of three parts: sensory registers, working memory, and long-term memory [see Figure 4.3].[2]

Figure 4.3: A Model of Human Memory

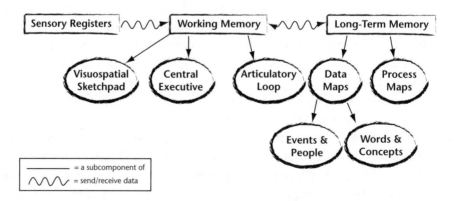

We receive incoming sensory data in our sensory registers. These registers minimally process this information. Their most important task is to send data into our working memory.

Working memory is sometimes called short-term memory because it stores and processes data only briefly as we use it to solve problems or respond to immediate situations. Our working memory has three subsystems.

- The *central executive* acts as a switchboard that controls the flow and processing of data. This component governs the system and makes executive decisions about information.

- The *sketchpad* briefly holds visual or spatial information we use to solve problems. Finding my way to a new location, I pull off the highway and consult my map. I then put the map away and pull back onto the highway. My visual sketchpad momentarily holds an image of the highway, the upcoming intersection, and the road onto which I must turn after the traffic light. This information does not go into my long-term memory. It sits briefly in my working memory.

- The *articulatory loop* stores and processes speech-based information temporarily as we use it. Its capacity is limited to what can be articulated in approximately two seconds. Imagine the recording device on your telephone's voice mail system. Someone leaving a message for you has thirty seconds to record a message. After that, the tape runs out and the recorder cuts the person off. The articulatory loop is a two-second tape! It can store about two seconds of information and then runs out of space. For most people living in Western societies, two seconds represents approximately seven units of data. For example, we can recall a seven-digit telephone number or a five-digit zip code. If we encounter longer sequences of words or numbers, we have difficulty remembering them.

Chunking strategies extend our working memory's capacity. If we chunk information into manageable units, our working memory can hold more data. Chunking means that categorized lists are recalled more easily than randomized information. More information can be processed because more data is contained in each unit. The limited number of chunks we can process are each rich in information rather than random, discrete bits of data.[3] If I am given sixty-six books of the Bible to remember, I will have great difficulty. I will process them much more easily if I can chunk these sixty-six books first into two categories—Old Testament and New Testament—and then chunk each of those categories into smaller categories.

While working memory is short and limited, long-term memory is virtually limitless. Adults can hold huge quantities of knowledge in their neural nets. Some of this knowledge is held in what we described in the previous chapter as process maps—networks of information that describe how procedures or sequences work. Other knowledge exists in what we called data maps. These contain memories of people, events, words, or concepts.

When we need knowledge to solve a problem or think about a situation, we retrieve it from our long-term memory and place it temporarily in our working memory. Since this working memory has a limited capacity, we can hold only so much information at any given time. Chunking strategies allow the working memory to retrieve and hold a more complex set of data than would be possible if it were working only with discrete bits of information [see Figure 4.4].

Figure 4.4: How Memory Works

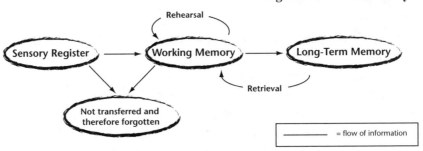

An understanding of these processes can be applied in many ways by Christian educators. Two very basic chunking applications utilize our sense of time and of space. A third capitalizes on the brain's natural sorting tendencies.

Chunking by Time. Time or chronology is a basic chunking strategy. Sunday school teachers often unknowingly use this approach. They chunk biblical history into large blocks of time. Much detail can be held in each chunk. Students are then able to recall more easily relationships between events and people. We speak, for example, of God's covenants with Adam, Noah, Abraham, David, and then the new covenant in Christ. Or we divide the New Testament into chunks of time: John the Baptist, Jesus, then Paul. All these are chunking strategies. Effective Sunday school teachers intentionally help their students to chunk material. They then check for how learners are holding this knowledge.

Zsavondra looked at the sixth-grade lesson materials that her Sunday school superintendent had just given her. She could see that she would be teaching about Moses and the Exodus for the next quarter. As she reviewed the material, she thought about how best to help her students learn these stories. She decided to use a chunking strategy already implicit in the quarterly curriculum.

At the beginning of the quarter, Zsavondra helped her students create a large chart that they hung on her classroom wall. Her chart chunked Moses' life into easily remembered blocks of time [see Figure 4.5].

Figure 4.5: Moses' Life—Zsavondra's Chunking Strategy

Birth and Childhood	Call to Lead Israel	Out of Egypt	Commandment and Covenant	Wandering in the Wilderness	Death

At the end of each class session, she and her students would add comments, Scripture verses, or pictures to the appropriate column. At the beginning of the next session, Zsavondra reviewed the chart. Her review helped learners recall where they were in Moses' timeline and what had already happened. Sometimes she would ask them what they thought would happen next as a prelude to her lesson. At the end of the quarter, her students could easily tell the story of Moses' life and remember important stories and people associated with Moses.

Many students in Zsavondra's class attended only irregularly. The chart and her weekly review of Moses' life helped these learners make connections and build a more comprehensive mental map of Moses and the Exodus. They did not have bits and pieces of the story. Zsavondra's map helped them see the whole picture as well as the parts.

Chunking by Space or Geography. Down the hall from Zsavondra's classroom, Bob was teaching the fourth-grade Sunday school class. His class was also studying Moses and the Exodus. Bob, however, took a different approach to chunking. Like Zsavondra, Bob helped his students create an oversized chart that they hung on the wall. His chart was organized according to geography rather than chronology, however [see Figure 4.6].

Figure 4.6: The Life of Moses—Bob's Chunking Strategy

Egypt	Sinai	Red Sea	Mountain of God	Wilderness	Death

Each week learners added words, names, or events to the chart. Sometimes they found connections between events or places and used a brightly colored marker to draw arrows between them. Next to the chart, Bob hung a map of the ancient Near East. Colorful yarn stretched between places on the map and columns on the chart.

Bob's chart was organized by space or geography rather than by time. Like Zsavondra's, it chunked material in a way that was engaging, interactive, and easily remembered.

Both Bob and Zsavondra taught children in Piaget's stage of concrete operations. Their use of maps, charts, colored yarn, hand-drawn pictures, and other concrete objects was especially effective with this age group.

Both Zsavondra and Bob used chunking strategies to help students see the big picture. Even children who only came one or two Sundays each month could understand the relationships between parts and the whole. They did not experience disconnected lessons filled with isolated incidents and stories. They perceived the flow of the whole story of Moses and the Exodus.

Sorting Strategies. Sorting strategies ask learners to separate different qualities, people, events, or ideas into categories. Similarities and differences or compare-and-contrast activities, for example, help learners organize new material and recall it more easily.

A Sunday school teacher asked her fifth-grade students to compare Jerusalem to a major city near them. How were they the same? How were they different? [See Figure 4.7.]

Figure 4.7: How Is Denver Like Jerusalem?

Denver	Jerusalem

She then used this list as a bridge into her lesson on life in first-century Jerusalem. Her question invited learners to think about something they already knew—a city near them—and compare it to something unfamiliar—Jerusalem. Her students began by thinking they knew almost nothing about Jerusalem. By the time they finished, they realized they already knew a great deal that they could apply to the lesson. This is the essence of Piaget's assimilation. Learners massaged new information into what they already knew.

Listing advantages and disadvantages is another sorting strategy. In studying the life of Moses, one teacher asked students to compare life in Egypt to life in the wilderness [see Figure 4.8]. The lists helped students understand the story in a new light and better remember key facts about the Exodus.

Figure 4.8: Comparing Life in Egypt to Life in the Wilderness

Advantages of Life in Egypt	Disadvantages of Life in Egypt
Advantages of Life in the Wilderness	**Disadvantages of Life in the Wilderness**

Chunking strategies are rarely used alone. They are almost always combined with spatial and bridging strategies. Chunking, therefore, is a preliminary task that helps Sunday school teachers prepare for a lesson or activity that will involve other strategies.

The power of chunking—like that of the other cognitive strategies—lies not in the format itself but in the collaborative nature of learners interacting with the subject matter and each other. The remaining cognitive strategies build on this characteristic and extend its effectiveness.

Spatial Strategies

Spatial strategies display information visually. Visual displays have at least three advantages. First, we learn by simultaneously understanding both the parts and the whole. Spatial strategies help learners map out the big picture and also see how parts interrelate. It is easier to know how parts fit when we have the big picture. These strategies serve as a kind of telescopic lens, allowing learners to see the big picture but also zoom in to a particular detail. Second, spatial strategies provide a stable framework into which lots of detail can be added. Third, they display the connections between various parts, helping students integrate knowledge and see relationships.

Spatial strategies can be used both for assimilation and for accommodation. They help learners structure unfamiliar knowledge into a new mental model. If students already have the big picture, these strategies allow them to add a large array of additional information.

Spatial Displays and Our Mental Geography. These strategies are all about the visual display of information in a spatial field. They are a powerful learning tool because the brain naturally has a spatial orientation.

The brain is always operating in a spatial, physical context. Whatever we do, we are bodies in physical space. This spatial context plays a crucial role in memory.[4] In a concrete way, the brain thinks, knows, and remembers spatially. Consequently spatial displays of knowledge and events create powerful learning. They tap into how the brain naturally knows and remembers.

We are always moving in physical space. What we learn when we are moving physically is usually easily recalled. When we go to the grocery store, we seldom have to consult a map to find the milk or bread. We automatically remember the aisle for the cereal or coffee. We did not consciously try to memorize this information. Few of us take home a map of the store and study it intently, expecting to be quizzed on where to find the canned green beans. The connection between memory and physical movement allows us to learn and remember this information quickly.

Contrast this with how much effort goes into sitting at a desk or table trying to memorize words or concepts that lie flat on the page before us. Robert and Jonathan labor over their lists of spelling words every night. Such learning is laborious as well as tedious. It is also not efficient, as most test-takers will attest. When we sit memorizing a list of words or concepts that lie flat on a page, we are not accessing our spatial awareness. We may, in fact, not even be aware we are a physical body. We are completely in our heads. Paradoxically, learning and knowing are most difficult when we are in our heads and not our bodies. Learning is quite literally a matter of mind and muscle, brain and body. Our sons, for example, find it easier to recall spelling words when they add the simple physical movement of writing to their mental rehearsal.

Spatial cognitive strategies span a wide range of tools and techniques [see Figure 4.9].

Figure 4.9: Spatial Strategies

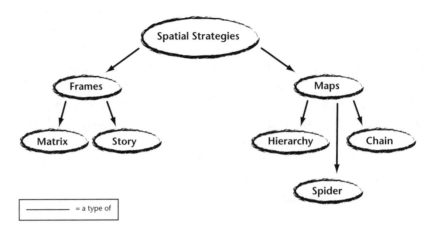

Two of the most common spatial strategies are frames and concept maps.

Frames. Frames are particularly useful when Christian educators want to help students see the big picture and not become lost in details. Frames visually display lots of information in a comprehensive and interconnected manner. Two common types of framing strategies are the matrix and the story frame.

A matrix frame is a chart consisting of columns and rows. Usually both the rows and columns are labeled. Information can then be entered into the slots. A story frame tries to capture the essential elements of a story's plot and characters. The rows and columns represent different people (rows) in the story and the columns represent plot sequences or moves.

When class members chose a short book on Paul's life and ministry as their quarterly study, Jerri wondered how she would teach her adult Sunday school class. She had read the book several times. But each time she became confused about Paul's missionary journeys. They all ran together in her mind. She had a hunch that others in the class would have the same difficulty. She decided she would display Paul's journeys in a simple story frame. It looked like Figure 4.10.

Working with her story frame, Jerri began to see relationships and interconnections. Some cities and people appeared in more than one journey, which made it easy to confuse them. But the frame helped her see events and places in their proper relationships to each other. The frame also helped Jerri perceive the big picture of Paul's ministry. With this big picture in mind, it was easier to remember specific events, people, and places.

Class members "tinkered" with Jerri's original map, reorganizing some of the columns and adding other features. Each week, Jerri used the story frame as an aid to group discus-

Figure 4.10: Jerri's Chart of Paul's Missionary Journeys

	People	Places	Events	Reference in the Book of Acts	Related Epistle Letter
First Journey					
Second Journey					
Third Journey					

sion. The frame actually served as a prompt that helped quieter class members contribute their thoughts. Long after her class finished their study of Paul, members still commented on how meaningful and insightful Jerri's class had been.

Pastor Susan was preparing for her weekly confirmation class. This week's topic was the atonement: What was the purpose of Jesus' death on the cross? As Susan prepared for her class, she felt the material was likely to be too abstract and distant for her students. How could she help them understand what the chapter's authors were trying to say? On a sheet of newsprint, she drew a simple matrix frame and began to complete its slots [see Figure 4.11].

Figure 4.11: Pastor Susan's Matrix Frame

Theory	Major Thinker	Basic Ideas	Scripture References	Implications/ Consequences for Me

She introduced the matrix frame to her confirmands as a way they could understand what the chapter was trying to say and how it applied to them. The frame focused their discussion. Students seemed less confused by the chapter's heavily theological and doctrinal language. Following the closing prayer, one student turned and said to Susan, "Thanks. This was the first time I really understood why Jesus had to die on the cross."

Concept Maps. Mind or concept mapping also graphically displays concepts and relationships. Concept maps, like frames, capitalize on how the brain naturally uses spatial prompts to think, learn, and remember. Most mind maps consist of bubbles and lines. Concepts, events, facts, or persons are written inside the bubble. The line defines the relationships between the bubbles. A legend explains what the line represents.

Concept maps are particularly useful when the primary instructional goal is for learners to understand key concepts and their relationships. On the other hand, if factual detail is more important, then frames are the better strategy. While a story or matrix frame can hold large amounts of detail, concept maps have a limited carrying capacity for detail. They are best used to illustrate relationships.

Frames and maps differ in another way as well. Frames provide multiple pathways between different facts or concepts. Maps, however, usually display only one connectional pathway. A frame involves a gridlike arrangement with intersecting slots. A map, on the other hand, highlights specific relationships between distinct concepts, facts, or events. Since concept maps highlight specific relationships, they are ideal for stating propositions.

Three basic mind or concept maps are: chain, hierarchy, and spider maps. Chain maps describe step-by-step procedures or actions. Hierarchy maps display major concepts and their subparts. Spider maps present key information that is related to a central idea, person, or event.

Patti Catron taught Mt. Olive Church's elementary Sunday school class. Patti thought her students should learn the books of the Bible. So, she invited them to help her create a hierarchy map of the Bible on newsprint.

Over the course of the year, students kept adding detail to their map. Patti would remind students about the map each week. Often she would begin her lesson by asking them to locate their lesson on the map or create a new link if they could not find their book or topic. By the end of the year, her map looked something like Figure 4.12.

Figure 4.12: Patti's Hierarchy Map of the Bible

Other teachers often commented on how well Patti's children could locate books of the Bible or find where particular people or events were mentioned. Patti's hierarchy map created a structure that allowed students to recall and remember large amounts of biblical material. Patti's secret was her attention not just to what students were learning but to how they were learning and knowing it.

Chain maps list in a step-by-step manner all the stages in a particular sequence or procedural activity. An example of a chain map is found in Figure 4.13 (on page 74). Each step in creating an advance organizer is listed in a sequential manner. Chain maps allow students to remember more easily the steps in a process or sequence.

Spider maps simply display the relationship between several ideas or concepts. An example of a spider map is found in Figure 4.1 (on page 62). Spider maps help learners understand basic relationships. As can be seen from Figure 4.1, however, they do not have a large carrying capacity for information.

All these maps capitalize on the brain's natural capacity to create a spider web of knowing. They display knowledge in a way that mirrors the brain's own neural networking.

Relationship Between Chunking and Spatial Strategies. Spatial strategies depend on prior chunking. Once instructors or learners have chunked material into large categories, they can further process it into either frames or concept maps. Chunking is therefore a necessary precondition to preparing both frames and maps. While it can stand alone, chunking's capacity to carry more information or to deepen learning is enhanced when it is wedded to spatial strategies such as frames and maps.

Bridging Strategies

Bridging strategies constitute a third category of cognitive strategies. Bridges span bodies of water, railroads, or natural chasms. In the same way, bridging strategies help students connect previous knowledge and new material. They bridge bodies of information that otherwise might remain separated. Two basic bridging strategies are advance organizers and metaphors. Christian educators frequently overlook these strategies. Yet they are particularly helpful due to the nature of participation in religious education and faith formation programs.

Participation in religious education is often sporadic and irregular. Sunday school teachers consequently resign themselves to approaching each Sunday's lesson as a free-standing unit. They assume learners will have no prior exposure to the week's themes and topics. They teach as if students were not in class last week and will not return next Sunday. Sunday school instruction thus passes from lesson to lesson, quarter to quarter, year to year, with students noticing almost no connections between what they previously studied and what they are now learning.

When learners experience no obvious connections between topics, they approach each lesson mindlessly. They do not think about what they already know and how it might intersect with what they are now learning. Yet two of the most important variables in instructional design, as we have seen from Piaget, are what learners already know and how that knowledge is organized.

Learning in general—and assimilation in particular—depends on massaging new information into what we already know. The brain uses existing mental maps as frameworks into which it can add new details. As we saw in our discussion of the brain, we do not learn by creating individual file bins for each new fact. We learn by linking new information into existing networks of memory and knowledge. Learners incorporate new knowledge into old knowledge.

Religious instruction, however, often fails to help learners activate their prior knowledge. Mobilizing this prior knowledge enhances student learning and long-term recall.

Bridging strategies intentionally activate prior knowledge so that new learning occurs with greater depth and power.

Advance Organizers. Advance organizers connect new knowledge to what learners already know. They remind students of similarities between prior knowledge and new information, thus encouraging them to transfer or apply what they already know to something new.

An advance organizer is more than an introductory statement or activity. It is not an icebreaker or an opening exercise. Advance organizers have a particular structure. Their effectiveness depends on this format. Using these steps, church educators can create advance organizers that help learners activate prior knowledge and deepen present learning [see Figure 4.13].

Figure 4.13: Using an Advance Organizer

Teachers first study their lesson or unit to identify where students might have prior knowledge of the topic. Has it been previously taught in earlier grades? Next, the instructor lists the lesson's key ideas and writes an advance organizer to emphasize similarities between the new lesson and what students have previously learned. For the advance organizer to work effectively, teachers must follow the same sequence in instruction as they use in the organizer.

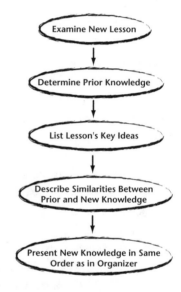

Chuck Martinez is preparing to teach his Sunday school class about Abraham and Sarah. Looking at the curriculum overview, he sees that his fifth- and sixth-grade class studied Abraham and Sarah two years earlier. Looking at the guide, he notes the themes and Scriptures they would have learned during that year. He next looks at his upcoming lesson and lists its principle themes. Armed with this information, he writes an advance organizer for Sunday's session:

> *Today we are going to begin several lessons about Abraham and Sarah. The last time you studied Abraham and Sarah in Sunday school, you learned about how God called them to leave their home country and travel to the land God promised them. Their trust in God was a model of what being faithful to God looks like. Today and in the next few lessons we are going to learn more about Abraham and Sarah. We will be hearing again some of what you learned before. We will also learn more about their journey in the Promised Land, about some of the people they met, and about how God made a covenant with them. We will learn about how God is a God who covenants or enters into personal relationships with*

us. And we will learn more about how Abraham and Sarah's faith in God shows us how we too can be faithful to God.

On Sunday, Chuck begins his class by reading his advance organizer. He then asks students what they remember about Abraham and Sarah from Sunday school, worship, or vacation Bible school. The advance organizer and discussion serve as a springboard into the lesson. Chuck Martinez activates his students' prior knowledge before introducing new material. By activating their prior knowledge, Chuck has made it easier for his students to incorporate new knowledge into what they already know.

Metaphor. We usually think of metaphors in connection with poetry, not teaching and learning. Metaphors are much more than just literary devices, however. They are a powerful tool for Christian learning and faith formation, as any preacher knows.

This bridging strategy actually includes analogies and similes as well as metaphors. All three literary devices compare two unlike things so as to highlight a relationship between them. "Like a rose opening to the sun, our souls open to God," for example, is a simile. A metaphor, on the other hand, might be: "Jesus is the new Elijah who crosses waters, raises dead children, and miraculously multiplies food." A high school English teacher might object to lumping these literary terms into a single category, but educational researchers have typically treated them as one category.

Like advance organizers, metaphors compare something familiar to something unfamiliar. Both advance organizers and metaphors rely on similarities across topics, concepts, events, or people. Metaphors differ from advance organizers in important ways, however. An advance organizer is usually more literal and contains much more information than a metaphor, which is usually figurative and brief. Whereas an advance organizer relies on specific prior instructional knowledge, a metaphor is usually based on general knowledge or perceptions.

Furthermore, most instructional strategies foster assimilation rather than accommodation. Metaphors, on the other hand, can produce rapid accommodation. They are an ideal strategy when the goal is accommodation rather than assimilation. Metaphors can almost immediately alter learners' mental maps. Jesus' parables and sayings consistently use metaphors to restructure how listeners see themselves and their world: The reign of God is like a mustard seed. God is the forgiving parent who rushes out to welcome the prodigal child.

Throughout this book, a variety of metaphors have been used to aid learning: The three parts of the human brain are like your finger poked through a bagel with a sheet of paper atop it. Accommodation is like teachers trying to find a new restaurant in a strange city. The short-term memory's articulatory loop is a two-second tape on your voice-mail recorder. Each compared something familiar to something new. They bridged between old and new knowledge.

One does not have to be a poet to create metaphors. Religious language relies extensively on metaphor. Usually metaphors are already embedded either in the biblical theme being taught or in the curriculum materials. Church educators who look with fresh eyes at their materials might discover powerful metaphors they could use in their classrooms. For example, the Psalms begin with a metaphor: the righteous person is a tree planted by streams of living water.

Maja sat down to prepare her junior high Sunday school lesson on Jesus' parable of the lost sheep. Looking out her high-rise window, she was aware that few of her students had ever seen sheep, let alone a shepherd. How could she make this parable more real for her students? Doodling on her note pad, she thought of different occupations with which her students might be familiar. These included everything from firefighters to bus drivers. Eventually, she thought she might explore further some of the attributes of firefighters. She drew a simple matrix and began to fill in some of the slots [see Figure 4.14].

Figure 4.14: Maja's Metaphor Worksheet

	Shepherd	Firefighter
Attributes		
Relationships		

Her mind wandered to the attributes of firefighters who rush into burning buildings, seeking trapped or injured victims. She began to think about the relationships between firefighters and those they save. Gradually, her chart had comments and observations in each slot.

On Sunday, she introduced her lesson on Jesus' parable of the lost sheep by saying, "Jesus is the good firefighter who risks his own life, rushing back into a burning building to seek and save one last person trapped behind flames and smoke." She invited her students to list briefly all the qualities and attributes of firefighters. Then she continued by observing, "We may not know much about sheep and shepherds. But we do know about firefighters and burning buildings. As we hear today's lesson, let's think about how the good shepherd is like a good firefighter."

CONCLUSION

Keeping in touch with teaching means keeping in touch with cognitive learning strategies. Thanks to cognitive science and Piaget's research, teachers have available to them practical, concrete tools for helping learners read, learn, mark, and inwardly digest God's revelation in Jesus Christ. These cognitive strategies empower teachers both to transmit and to transform the Christian faith entrusted to them.

Deepening Your Learning

1. Find a quiet spot where you can reflect. Think back to your own religious educational experience. What biblical stories or theological concepts are most memorable or vivid to you? What in the way you processed these stories or concepts made them such powerful memories? What can you learn from this experience to help make biblical material or theological beliefs vivid for your students?

2. Experiment with using your body to learn and remember. Rather than think about the previous question while you are sitting in a chair, reflect on it while you are walking, jogging, or exercising. What is available to you as you move physically that was not available to you when you were just sitting? How were these two experiences of remembering different? What can you learn about this difference to improve your teaching?

3. Read back through this chapter and create a spatial strategy that summarizes its key points. Can you construct a matrix frame for this chapter? A concept map?

4. Look back at the previous pages and write an advance organizer for this chapter. What did you focus on? What skills did you use? How could you use these skills to design an advance organizer for your next Sunday school class or small group?

5. We have used several metaphors for the brain. It is a neural net, a spider web, a finger-through-the-bagel. Be playful and design a completely fresh metaphor for learning and the brain. What do you learn about yourself as you do this?

Endnotes

1 See *Instructional Design: Implications From Cognitive Science,* by Charles K. West, James A. Farmer, and Phillip M. Wolff (Prentice Hall, 1991). This chapter relies both on their text and my experiences in their course "Instructional Design" when I was a graduate student at the University of Illinois at Urbana-Champaign.

2 See *Learning and Memory: Major Ideas, Principles, Issues, and Applications,* by Robert W. Howard (Praeger, 1995), pages 59-68.

3 See *Fundamentals of Cognitive Psychology,* fifth edition, by Henry C. Ellis and R. Reed Hunt (WCB Brown & Benchmark, 1993), pages 82-83.

4 See *Making Connections: Teaching and the Human Brain,* by Renate Nummela Caine and Geoffrey Caine (Association for Supervision and Curriculum Development, 1991), pages 38-40.

CHAPTER FIVE

Journeys
and Resting Places

Moral and Faith Development

Jean Piaget sought to understand how our thinking changes over time. Piaget's research points Christian educators toward the importance of focusing not only on what learners know, but also on how they know it—on the mental operations they use to process, store, and recall information. As we saw in the previous chapter, Piaget's insights and neuroscience's discoveries together point toward practical strategies for Christian teaching and faith formation.

But faith involves more than cognitive knowledge of God and Scripture. Faith also includes moral commitments and ethical decision-making. It encompasses personal faithfulness and intimacy with God through Christ in the Spirit. Our baptism calls us to the love, knowledge, and service of God and neighbor. Jesus said, " 'You shall love the Lord your God with all your heart, and with all your soul, and with all your mind.' This is the greatest and first commandment. And a second is like it: 'You shall love your neighbor as yourself.' On these two commandments hang all the law and the prophets" (Matthew 22:37-40).

Christian faith involves the totality of our lives: our minds and bodies, our hearts and wills. To change one of these is to change all the others. New knowledge challenges us to make new commitments. Unexpected moral dilemmas cause us to rethink previous religious understandings. A profound religious experience can even change how we physically carry ourselves in our bodies. Wrapped about all this is the endless mystery of a God who works through grace to make us alive in Christ [see Figure 5.1].

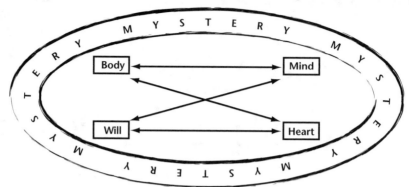

This dynamic dance between mind, body, will, and heart describes Christian sanctification. We are always giving the more of what we know about ourselves to the more we know of God. For this reason, Christian faith is a journey, not a destination. It is a verb, not a noun; a process, not a static condition.

John Wesley spoke of this journey as "going on to perfection." Our conversion is not a one-time event after which nothing changes. Throughout our lives we are claiming what we profess in our baptism. The Spirit continually invites us to deeper transformations of our love, knowledge, and service to God and neighbor.

How do Piaget's stages relate to these changes in our moral behavior and faith formation? If body, will, mind, and heart are interconnected, how does our moral reasoning change as we mentally grow and mature? Do the structures of faith undergo transformations similar to those Piaget discovered in mental development? If mental development follows predictable stages, then do moral commitments and faith relationships proceed along similar timetables?

John Wesley spoke of prevenient grace, the grace that goes before us and prepares the way for our receiving God's justifying grace. Prevenient grace, Wesley thought, works quietly within us long before we become aware of God's loving presence in our lives.

Beneath the earth's surface lie enormous tectonic plates that ride upon the planet's molten core. Over time these plates move and shift. For a long, long time, these changes happen invisibly and silently beneath the earth. Then, one day, their pent-up pressures explode into an earthquake that rumbles through the ground and shakes the landscape. Like the earth's tectonic plates, God's prevenient grace works silently beneath the surface of our lives, preparing us for a transforming encounter with the God who loves us and calls us forth from death to new life in Christ.

Perhaps God acts preveniently in our lives through the stages of mental, moral, and faith development, preparing us for growth in Christ. Like the earth's tectonic plates, developmental tasks and stages slowly shift and change beneath the surface of our lives.

Shifts in one plate or developmental task create pressure on the others. Pressure builds up until visible, concrete transformations explode into our lived experience.

Keeping in touch with teaching means keeping in touch with what researchers are discovering about Piaget and cognitive development. But Piaget alone is not enough for faithful teaching and learning. Christian educators also keep in touch with insights into moral growth and faith formation.

The most extensive research on moral development has been done by Lawrence Kohlberg. Kohlberg's research led him to propose several stages of moral development that parallel Piaget's stages of cognitive development. James Fowler has undertaken a similar task with faith development. Like Kohlberg, Fowler uses Piaget's theory as a foundation for his work.

Stages of Moral Development

Kohlberg based his work on Piaget's analysis of cognitive development. These roots distinguish Kohlberg's approach from alternative understandings of moral growth. Some theories of moral development believe that individuals are basically good. Our inborn goodness will emerge on its own if we are allowed to unfold naturally. Moral behavior is like a flower bud that opens effortlessly to the sun. The French philosopher Jean-Jacques Rousseau held to this maturationist position, which still has its advocates in religious and public educational circles. Other theories of moral development emphasize cultural transmission and the direct teaching of moral values or behavior. Children are inherently amoral unless particular virtues are introjected into them. A moral person can be built through intentional instruction and ethical teaching.

Kohlberg rejects both these positions. He instead opts for a middle path. Moral development does not unfold effortlessly from inside ourselves. Nor is it imposed externally by forces outside the self. Moral behavior develops as internal biological processes encounter external situations, people, or events. Just as Piaget believed that new mental operations develop through encounters between internal biological changes and external challenges, Kohlberg thought that moral reasoning developed as inner changes met outer challenges.

Kohlberg, like Piaget, was interested in the actual process of moral reasoning rather than in its contents or outcomes. He wanted to know *how* we reason morally, not *what* conclusions we reach. Moral development, he concluded, parallels cognitive development. Like Piaget's cognitive development, Kohlberg's moral development occurs in a series of stages that are sequential, invariable, and hierarchical.

Kohlberg believed that individuals pass through three levels of moral reasoning. Each level has two stages of development within it [see Figure 5.2]. He named these levels for the degree to which people conform to external moral conventions or expectations: preconventional, conventional, and postconventional.[1]

Figure 5.2: Kohlberg's Levels of Moral Development

Level	Stage	Description
Preconventional		Moral reasoning based on physical or quasi-physical needs
	One	Oriented to punishment
	Two	Oriented to rewards
Conventional		Moral reasoning based on meeting role expectations of others
	Three	Avoid disapproval of significant others
	Four	Conform to please peers, group
Postconventional		Moral reasoning based on larger principles
	Five	Conform to what the whole society agrees is good
	Six	Follow own inner principles, values

Preconventional Moral Reasoning. During this level of development, moral values reside in external, quasi-physical events or actions rather than in people or abstract standards.

Within this level, the first stage of moral reasoning is oriented toward avoiding punishment. When asked why she doesn't go outside the yard to play in the street, a five-year-old says, "Mommy will give me a time-out if I leave the yard."

At the second stage, children are oriented toward satisfying their own needs. Moral reasoning acquires a "you scratch my back and I'll scratch yours" quality. A child obeys moral rules in order to earn a reward.

Children at this stage of moral development have a highly developed sense of fairness. What applies to one person applies equally to someone else. As our younger son constantly reminded me when he was this age, "It's not fair that Robert gets to stay up later than I do."

Conventional Moral Reasoning. Conventional moral reasoning emerges about the same time as Piaget's formal operations. Quasi-concrete objects like physical rewards and punishments are no longer the focus of moral reasoning. Now, other people are the basis for moral decision-making.

A youth entering Kohlberg's stage three can understand and enter into another person's perspective. Hence other people's opinions and intentions play an important role in moral decision-making. Children want to conform to the conventional expectations that others have of them. Enrique does the "right thing" because he does not want to face the disapproval of his peers or significant adults around him. "What would Grandpa think if I ..." he wonders. His actions are moral if they conform to others' expectations. Children are motivated to please the people who matter in their lives and not to disappoint them.

In stage four, the ability to take another perspective remains critical. Now, however, the person is able to take the perspective of a whole group or society and not just another individual. Appeals to "law and order" resonate strongly in this stage. One avoids behavior that might result in social censure. As a result, people at this stage are strongly oriented toward "doing their duty."

Postconventional Moral Reasoning. The most mature level is postconventional moral reasoning. This level also includes two stages: social contract and universal principles. After age twenty-five, most adults have left home and entered the world of work and civic responsibility. They have experienced conflicting values and ambiguous moral choices. They can see the shortcomings and limitations of previously clear moral rules and guidelines.

Young adults also have experiences of sustained responsibility for the welfare of others. They are responsible for the upbringing of their own children. They may have growing responsibilities for aging parents. These experiences create opportunities for them to define their own guiding moral principles apart from the conventional relationships in which they were earlier embedded.

This approach focuses on utility and individual rights. Young adults can recognize the relativity and limitations of social rules and laws. But they still uphold them in the name of utility. These rules are part of the social contract by which we all agree to live together as a society. The concern is for the greatest good for the greatest number of people. Responding to Ida Mae's invitation to take some office supplies from the company storeroom, Joey's answer is no longer: "What would my father think?" Nor is it "What will my coworkers think?" Instead he says, "I have to act responsibly just like everyone else does, so that everybody in the company can do well."

According to Kohlberg, few people reach the sixth stage of universal principles. Persons who reach this stage are oriented primarily to what their own conscience demands of them. They make moral decisions based on self-chosen but universal principles of love and justice. Martin Luther King Jr. or Mahatma Gandhi represent this stage of moral development.

Kohlberg believed that interaction with other people plays a decisive role in our passage from one stage to the next. As we observe people modeling the next stage's moral reasoning, we are stretched to move forward ourselves.

Kohlberg also argued for the principle of readiness. We can usually reason only at our own level of moral development and no more than one stage above us. Our chances for moving upward are enhanced when we are challenged by moral reasoning slightly above our own stage. But if the gap is too great, we cannot rise to the challenge.

Kohlberg's model, like Piaget's, depends on a principle of conflict and resolution. We grow when we encounter experiences that conflict with our present moral roadmaps and ethical principles. These dissonant experiences challenge us to redefine ourselves and our understanding of ethical or moral behavior. Moral dilemmas and discussion about moral issues inevitably stretch us beyond our current stage of moral development.

STAGES OF FAITH DEVELOPMENT

James Fowler's father was a Methodist pastor, and young Fowler grew up listening to many people's stories of faith, loss, and rebirth. After completing his graduate coursework at Harvard, Fowler worked at Interpreters' House, Carlyle Marney's retreat center. In this setting, he became captivated by stories of faith that people told. These experiences, plus his study with Kohlberg at Harvard, form the background for his seven-stage theory of faith development [see Figure 5.3].[2]

Figure 5.3: Fowler's Stages of Faith Development

Number	Name	Age	Description
0	Undifferentiated	Birth–2	Acquire preimages of God, self, and world
1	Intuitive-Projective	2–7	Active imagination and fantasy Project self into story and narrative
2	Mythic-Literal	7–12	Emphasis on fact and literal meanings Ability to tell stories and enter imaginatively into them
3	Synthetic-Conventional	12–18	Synthesize previous stories into a personal story of one's life Internalize norms and values of peer or primary identity group
4	Individuative-Reflective	18–40	Think critically about faith they have created at previous stage Separate own beliefs from beliefs of groups, significant others
5	Conjunctive	Midlife	Reintegration of values, beliefs left behind earlier Tolerance for ambiguity, paradox
6	Universalizing	40+	Decenter self by centering on God Faith that looks beyond all boundaries and includes all people, cultures, religions

Undifferentiated Faith. Fowler calls his initial stage undifferentiated faith. This stage begins at birth and lasts until age two. As we have learned from brain research and Piaget's observations, infants lack the mental operations necessary for thinking conceptually. Nonetheless, infants are forming a basic sense of trust. They are also acquiring preimages of God and the kind of world we live in.

Brain research suggests that powerful images formed early in life have a profound effect on our emotional responses. Long before our hippocampus develops, the amygdala is busy categorizing images that have a strong negative or positive emotional charge. The imprint of these strong, emotionally charged images, symbols, and experiences will shape our lifelong faith experience. These early experiences form the foundation upon which later religious faith is constructed.

Dagmar has a strong negative reaction whenever someone mentions God. Dagmar's image of God is built from experiences and memories of her father. He was a factory worker who came home drunk each afternoon and physically abused Dagmar and her mother. Although her father died when she was three, Dagmar's amygdala still sends out an alarm when it picks up incoming signals bearing even a slight resemblance to these experiences. References to God—especially a God who condemns and punishes us—trigger Dagmar's amygdala. Preimages from Dagmar's early life have produced an emotional template that inhibits her adult spiritual journey. These preimages and patterns are so deep and so early that Dagmar is hardly aware of them. Their invisibility makes it difficult for her to examine and revise them.

Intuitive/Projective Faith. Between ages two and seven, approximately, children develop what Fowler labels an intuitive/projective faith. This stage roughly corresponds to Piaget's preoperational child. Children acquire language and begin to understand symbols. They are basically egocentric and cannot take another person's perspective. Because their sense of cause-and-effect is weak, they have active imaginations. Lacking the kind of logic that makes it possible to question perceptions and stories, the child's mind is "religiously pregnant."

According to Fowler, stories, images, and symbols have particular importance for faith development. Because fantasy and imagination are so active, children enter into stories and make their own meanings. These meanings can often be individual and illogical. Since children do not think as adults do, they can misinterpret or misunderstand what these stories mean. Images and stories we internalize at this age have a powerful negative or positive effect in later faith development.

Mack has no interest in church or religion. Whenever you speak with him, he always returns to the same story: When he was six years old his baby sister died. The day she died, Mack's mother told him, "God and the angels came and got your sister. They needed her more than we do." Consequently, Mack associates God and the angels with death and the ripping away of a beloved baby sister who had done nothing to deserve death. "If that's who God is," he says, "I don't want anything to do with him." Mack internalized a story that continues to play a powerful negative role in his faith formation.

The danger of intuitive/projective faith is that the child's imagination becomes fixated on images of fear and destruction. Another danger comes from adults who exploit this stage's openness to story and symbol to reinforce religious or moral taboos. When this happens to children, they have difficulty moving past a narrow doctrinal rigidity even as adults.

Christian educators therefore have a special responsibility when working with intuitive/projective children. They can share stories and images that are life-opening and sustain faith. Or they can insist on conceptual orthodoxy and preach stories that give rise to later rigidity and fear.

Sunday school teachers can best help intuitive/projective children by encouraging them to enter imaginatively into Bible stories and parables. These stories become a rich resource out of which adolescents and adults can create a meaningful faith. Christian educators have a responsibility to create symbol- and story-rich environments for this age group while not prematurely providing narrow conceptual or doctrinal interpretations of what these stories must mean.

Mythic/Literal Faith. Fowler's next stage is mythic/literal faith, which occurs roughly between ages seven and twelve. Individuals are now capable of Piaget's concrete operations, and the previous stage's fantasy and imagination give way to concrete literalism. Children work hard to distinguish make-believe from real. They insist on demonstration and proof. These children are also interested in learning the lore and stories of their particular group, church, or family. They take these stories pretty much at face value. They can also tell and retell these stories themselves. Finally, as we saw from Kohlberg, these children have a finely developed sense of fairness and reciprocity.

Christian educators can use story, drama, art, and music to make biblical narratives become both concrete and memorable. On the other hand, an excessive insistence on fairness can result in works righteousness and perfectionism.

Ironically, this stage's love of narrative and story sows the seeds for the transition to Fowler's next stage. As children begin to notice conflicts both within and between stories, they experience a crisis that propels them forward.

Synthetic/Conventional Faith. Beginning generally between ages twelve and eighteen, synthetic/conventional faith emerges. Its development parallels the appearance of Piaget's formal operations. For the first time, adolescents can think about their thinking. They are able to think about familiar stories in new ways. Adolescents now use these stories to construct a personal narrative telling who they are and what they will become. Having listened to stories about other people and places, they now construct their own personal story. This story is ultimately about their hopes and dreams. It tells them who they are. For, in the last analysis, we are the stories we tell.

Adolescents are also keenly sensitive to how others perceive them. Having arrived at Piaget's stage of formal operations, they can take multiple perspectives—including how others are seeing them. Hence, peer pressure plays a powerful role in faith formation. For Kohlberg, this marks the emergence of conventional moral reasoning, which is sensitive to how others judge one's choosing and acting. Fowler sees a similar process unfold in the faith development of adolescents. How they articulate their faith is strongly influenced by social pressures and the need to belong and feel included. Not by accident, confirmation, baptism, or renewal of one's baptismal vows usually occur during these years.

According to Fowler, many people remain at the level of synthetic/conventional faith. They do not progress further. We have here a hint that Fowler's later stages may not in fact be so much "stages" as "styles" of faith. They are ways adults live out their faith in the world regardless of age.

Individuative/Reflective Faith. Fowler's individuative/reflective faith has only a vague timeline. It may emerge as early as late adolescence or as late as midlife. An intense questioning of the conventional faith that the person previously constructed marks this stage. Adults at this stage question what they worked so hard to make their own in the previous stage. This stage is concerned with boundaries. Where do I stop and you begin? Where do the group's beliefs end and my beliefs begin? Adults begin to distinguish their own personal views from the beliefs of significant others.

Because the ability to think about thinking is now fully developed, adults often critically analyze the stories and symbols that previously nurtured them. Abstract meanings and concepts replace narrative and image. This brings a newfound capacity to understand and articulate one's faith. But it also brings a certain flattening out of religious experience. Faith can be too much in one's head and not enough in one's heart. Another hazard associated with this stage is an overconfidence in rational thinking that evaluates everything in terms of one's own egocentric rationality.

Conjunctive Faith. Adults are often propelled beyond the individuative/reflective faith by disillusionment and tragedy. Life's crises and complexities force adults to recognize that life is more than clear logic and abstract concepts. They begin to re-encounter the religious stories, symbols, and metaphors they thought they had left behind. This marks their entry into Fowler's next stage, conjunctive faith. This stage's task is to unify opposites and to bring back into wholeness parts of the self previously separated: heart and mind, spirit and body. Defeat and failure press many adults to look beyond an either/or outlook and to embrace life's mystery, paradox, and complexity.

A capacity for dialogue is especially important at this stage of faith development. If reality is multidimensional, the truth I experience must be interdependent with another's truth. Qualities such as vulnerability, receptivity, dialogue, and mutuality characterize conjunctive faith. Adults are fully committed to their own beliefs and also recognize these beliefs as partial, fragmentary, and in need of continual reassessment.

Universalizing Faith. According to Fowler's research, less than ten percent of the population ever reaches the stage of conjunctive faith. Less than one percent attains his final stage, universalizing faith. Those exemplifying universalizing faith include people like Dag Hammarskjold, Mother Teresa, Thomas Merton, or Martin Luther King Jr. Adults who arrive at universalizing faith are drawn there by God's providence, not their own intentions or efforts. They no longer place themselves at the center of their experience but instead put God at the center of their lives. They are able to negate themselves for the sake of affirming God. Yet, in this process, they themselves become more alive and vibrant.

Because they do not place themselves at the center of existence, they are able to commit themselves to an inclusive community that goes beyond all definitions of class, race, gender, or religion. Established religious communities often experience these persons as a subversive threat and try to eliminate or remove them from their midst. Thus, adults who reach this stage often become martyrs.

CRITICS OF KOHLBERG AND FOWLER

Several critics have taken issue with both Kohlberg and Fowler. Kohlberg's critics have objected to his assertion that his model is universally valid—that it applies not just to North Americans but to indigenous peoples in Latin America, Tibetan peasants, and everyone else. These critics argue that Kohlberg is imposing Western, middle-class values on diverse cultures.

Another criticism of Kohlberg's work has come from Carol Gilligan. Gilligan's research led her to propose that Kohlberg's model reflects a male bias. Men, Gilligan concludes, are socialized to an ethic of rights. Their upbringing encourages independence and separation. Hence they think in terms of individual rights and impartial justice. Women, on the other hand, are socialized into an ethic of care. They are socialized into interdependence and therefore think in terms of relationships and care. Kohlberg's interview method, in which he poses moral dilemmas and assesses how participants respond, favors a male ethic of rights while minimizing a female ethic of care and interdependence.

Fowler's model of faith development has been criticized as being not just a descriptive model of faith formation but a prescriptive one as well. Fowler assumes that faith development is something for which we should strive—that we should actively seek the higher stages of development.

Another criticism of Fowler's theory is that it contains no room for the idea of conversion. If our faith unfolds from one stage to the next from seemingly internal mechanisms, where is the place for conversion? For election? For grace?

Still other critics have asserted that Fowler's stages reflect primarily his own Methodist theology and beliefs. Some have complained that Fowler's adult stages are more "styles" than "stages." Indeed, Fowler's own research shows that many adults never attain the latter three stages of his model. What does it mean for the adult population to be so broadly distributed into stages that appear unrelated to age itself?

IMPLICATIONS FOR CHRISTIAN TEACHING

Despite these limitations of moral and faith development theories, Kohlberg and Fowler make important contributions to Christian teaching and faith formation. Keeping in touch with teaching requires keeping in touch with their theories.

Five Implications From Moral and Faith Development. At least five basic principles for Christian teaching and faith formation emerge from Kohlberg and Fowler.

First, faith involves the totality of life, not just assent to intellectual beliefs. How we articulate our beliefs is important, but intellectual assent to doctrines is only part of Christian faith. Christian teaching that limits itself to doctrinal or biblical instruction does a disservice to believers.

Second, Kohlberg and Fowler highlight the importance of dialogue in faith development. Both researchers use methods that rely on one-to-one interviews. Growing in faith never happens in isolation. It requires conversation partners. Dialogue and conversation are absolutely essential for faith formation. Our faith develops and grows in mutuality and partnership with others. Christian teaching is not a one-way monologue. It is a dialogue between partners in a community of faith who seek to grow together in the love of God and neighbor.

Third, we do not grow unless we encounter people whose moral reasoning and faith stories challenge and sometimes even contradict our own. These encounters encourage us to reexamine existing mental maps and moral rules of the road. Only when confronted by experiences that call into question how we have previously constructed our mental maps can we grow cognitively, morally, or spiritually. The diversity of Christian community also provides us with role models from whom we can learn. These role models lure us toward the next step in our spiritual, intellectual, or moral pilgrimage.

People do not grow spiritually when they continually place themselves in groups and communities where everyone thinks, acts, and behaves just like they do. We grow spiritually when we place ourselves in faith communities characterized by diversity rather than conformity, by unity rather than uniformity. Faith formation depends upon seeing our differences as a source of strength rather than as a deficit to correct.

Fourth, individuals develop morally and spiritually in environments characterized by high challenge and high support. Without the challenge of diversity, we stagnate. But without support, we downshift into our R-brain or have a schema attack. Nothing stops learning like fear. Fear-filled environments are characterized by criticism, blaming, negativity, and judgment. Faith formation and moral transformation occur when high-challenge environments are also high-support environments. Hospitality and a welcoming, forgiving spirit characterize a high-challenge/high-support learning community.

Fifth, we need stretching opportunities that challenge us to move up in our development. For most people, these stretching opportunities come in the form of conflict and crisis. As internal conflicts build up in our lives, we are propelled into the next developmental stage. The hard-won clarity of individuative/reflective faith comes into conflict with the mystery, paradox, and irrationality of middle adulthood, precipitating the transition to conjunctive faith. Kohlberg's research methods, for example, posed moral or ethical dilemmas and then invited participants to describe how they would resolve the situation.

As we saw in our discussion of the new science of the brain, the human brain seeks coherence. It looks for patterns of meaning and sensory experience. In the same way, life's confusing conflicts and puzzling dilemmas stretch us toward new patterns of coherence and meaning.

Perspective Transformation and Discovery Learning. Horizontal assimilation of new information is critical to our development. Many of the cognitive teaching strategies we discussed in the previous chapter are ideal for this task. But eventually we encounter new experiences that do not fit into our carefully constructed mental maps. We perceive discrepancies we previously overlooked. At these points of conflict and challenge, vertical accommodation occurs. We are stretched to revise and restructure our mental maps.[3]

The principles we have just named are especially crucial for accommodative or transformative learning. In other words, the basic teaching techniques for accommodative learning are strategies of dialogue and discovery learning. The Christian educator's goal is not to help learners add new facts and skills to an already existing knowledge base. Rather, educators support students as they question previously taken-for-granted assumptive viewpoints and discover new modes of understanding.

The classroom environment has to disturb learners' mental maps so that learners begin to acknowledge the limitations and shortcomings of their previous knowing and valuing. Because this acknowledgment is inherently scary, learners require significant support as they examine and revise their mental maps.

Once learners begin to doubt their previous schemas or mental maps, they enter a period of transition. They are betwixt and between. They have left their old maps. But they have not fully arrived at a new formulation. They are pilgrims on the way. Like all pilgrims, they need reliable guides. The teacher's role becomes absolutely crucial at this point.

Having left behind old rules of the road and abandoned inadequate maps, they begin to experiment with new, alternative beliefs, skills, understandings, or values. It is here that the role of direct teaching plays a crucial role. New structures of knowing and believing must be drawn forth and constructed. Learners cannot do this alone, in a vacuum. The instructor and group perform a valuable role in providing feedback, offering clarification and correction, and cementing into place a new, more adequate representation of God, world, and self.

Without this support, the learner may have abandoned one inadequate mental structure only to embrace another that is equally flawed, misunderstood, or misdirected. "When the unclean spirit has gone out of a person, it wanders through waterless regions looking for a resting place, but it finds none. Then it says, 'I will return to my house from which I came.' When it comes, it finds it empty, swept, and put in order. Then it goes and brings along seven other spirits more evil than itself, and they enter and live there; and the last state of that person is worse than the first" (Matthew 12:43-45).

Our next chapter will flesh out these strategies. It will provide concrete examples and techniques that Christian educators can use to foster high-challenge/high-support environments where accommodative learning flourishes. Keeping in touch with teaching involves keeping in touch with these skills, values, and tools.

Deepening Your Learning

1. On a sheet of paper draw a line length-wise across the page. At one end, write the word "Birth" and at the other end write "Death." This line is a timeline of your life. Using hatch marks, divide the line into equal units and write above each hatch mark your equivalent age from birth to whenever you expect your life to end. Then put your significant faith experiences on the timeline. Some experiences may be moments of spiritual growth. Others may be when you were in the doldrums or apathetic or angry at God. Reflect on your spiritual timeline in light of Fowler's stages of faith. What correlations do you see? What differences? What can you learn from your timeline that can help you be a better teacher or small-group leader?

2. How might Kohlberg and Fowler both be describing "styles" of faith and moral reasoning more than age-specific stages? Can you make a case for each position? Which seems the stronger argument to you? Why?

3. Describe a time when facing a moral or ethical dilemma resulted in your letting go of previous moral judgments and embracing a new ethical or moral standard. What was this experience like for you? In what ways were you different? In what ways were you the same?

4. Describe an educational setting that was both high-challenge and high-support for you. What factors created this context? What was its impact on you? How might remembering this experience help you create a similar learning environment for others?

ENDNOTES

1 See *The Psychology of Moral Development: The Nature and Validity of Moral Stages,* by Lawrence Kohlberg (Harper & Row, 1984).

2 See *Stages of Faith: The Psychology of Human Development and the Quest for Meaning,* by James W. Fowler (Harper & Row, 1981). In his book Fowler refers to undifferentiated faith as a "pre-stage," not as a stage, but for the sake of simplicity we will categorize all seven periods of development as stages.

3 For more on the concepts in this section see *The Dilemma of Enquiry and Learning,* by Hugh G. Petrie (University of Chicago Press, 1981).

CHAPTER SIX

Listening for Wisdom

Dialogue, Discussion, and the Transformation of Our Minds

We all have a powerful inclination not to change. A therapist friend once said to me that when people come for an initial interview she asks herself what these potential clients really want from life and how much effort they will put into not getting it. We are all good at not getting what we really want from life. Even when we know our mental maps and internal rules of the road are erroneous, we tenaciously cling to them. The most significant barrier to learning may be the brain's own mental terrain. Sometimes the ten percent of the brain that we "use" keeps the other ninety percent from doing what it knows is right!

Martin knows that his dominating, controlling behavior alienates committee members, yet he refuses to change these self-defeating patterns. Joy recognizes her tendency to overcommit her time and energy, but she continues saying yes to every invitation. Frannie, an adolescent in St. John's youth group, can describe the dangers of drug and alcohol abuse, but she remains on the same self-destructive path toward addiction. Adult Sunday school classes at Mt. Olive Church dread to see Connie show up. She is argumentative and critical. No opinions can be right if they do not agree with her predetermined views. All conversation stops when she enters the room.

Another name for this behavior is resistance. Resistance is the unconscious process of slowing down or blocking the learning process. It occurs when people become fearful of losing something important to them. Resistance allows people to manage their anxiety over the effects of choosing to think, act, or believe differently.

Resistance to Learning

Resistance itself is neither good nor bad. It simply is. On the one hand, resistance has a positive impact. It prevents us from giving up important values and truths too quickly. It encourages us to look before we leap. On the other hand, resistance can block learning. It locks us into limiting beliefs and behaviors.

Whenever people are learning, resistance is present. It never goes away. Resistance is especially present when learners are involved in what Piaget describes as accommodation—learning that restructures or significantly changes how we think and act. We are less likely to resist learning that adds new facts or more detail to our current assumptive worlds. But when learning invites us to transform the fundamental meaning-perspectives through which we make sense of our lives, resistance inevitably rears its head.

Piaget describes accommodation as a periodic developmental leap forward in how we structure our knowing and thinking. Kohlberg and Fowler also highlight developmental challenges that foster accommodation or the restructuring of our spiritual and moral knowledge. Christians refer to this basic restructuring of our thinking and acting as conversion. These experiences always generate resistance because they involve facing the unknown, suffering the loss of something precious or dear to us, or feeling inadequate as we try to master new behaviors or patterns of thought. As a consequence, we too can be "almost persuaded" like King Agrippa when our resistance holds us back (Acts 26:24-29).

Christian conversion can be a once-in-a-lifetime experience that comes with great power and drama. In other cases it is an ongoing process in which, throughout our lives, we are transformed again and again by the power of God's good news in Jesus Christ. When we experience these moments of conversion, we are not simply adding more details or facts to how we already understand ourselves and God. Our assumptive maps are turned upside down and we see the world through new eyes. The Greek word for repentance is *metanoia*. It literally means a change *(meta)* of mind *(nous)*.

The call to conversion always encounters resistance. This resistance is deeply rooted in our being. It arises, in part, from the very structure of how the brain learns and knows. If everything is a spider web of knowledge, then all we know is interconnected. To change one piece is to change the whole. Paradoxically, this constitutes both the strength and the weakness of human learning. Multiple connections allow the human brain to process and recall lots of information quickly. But these same multiple connections mean that the brain resists changing one piece of knowledge because it inevitably means reorganizing countless other interconnections across a whole web of memory and knowledge.

Recognizing Resistance

We know we are encountering resistance to learning when one or more of the following occurs:

1. Class members are totally silent and say nothing. If the Sunday school teacher or small-group leader is dealing with something important, silence is unnatural. Peo-

ple are sometimes silent because they feel so threatened by what they have heard that their feelings are blocked. Or they are afraid of what they might say if they begin to express themselves.

2. Group members go on the attack. They become angry and hostile. They lash out at the speaker, making accusations and questioning his or her Christian commitment.

3. Class members intellectualize about the topic. The conversation becomes increasingly abstract and disconnected from real life. They may be retreating into their heads because they are avoiding how they feel.

4. Group members moralize about a topic or situation. Whenever we hear a conversation filled with "ought" and "should," we are in the land of resistance. People have retreated from how they really feel into how they believe they should feel. They are not dealing with their true feelings but reverting to cliches.

5. Class members act excessively confused. Some confusion over new viewpoints or concepts is understandable. But when learners act confused after the group leader has explained things for the third or fourth time, participants are feigning confusion to avoid their anxieties.

The Power of Resistance

Christian educators and small-group leaders cannot afford to ignore resistance. It is too powerful a dynamic. Resistance can hold us captive. It can prevent us from giving the more of what we know of ourselves to the more we know of God.

We can learn about the power of resistance by looking at the history of mapmaking, or cartography. Resistance to changing actual physical maps of the world mirrors our resistance to changing our internal mental maps. One of the most famous examples is Henry Briggs's map showing California as an island. Briggs drew California as an island after receiving a sketchy report about two ships that passed on the west coast of North America. One ship told the other that it had discovered the western end of the much-sought but illusory Northwest Passage linking the Atlantic and Pacific Oceans. Briggs's map, published in 1625, even contained marginal notes explaining how he reached his conclusion that California was an island. After this error entered cartography in 1625, it remained a standard feature of many maps until nearly the American Revolution 150 years later. In 1747, King Ferdinand VII of Spain actually issued a royal decree stating that California was not an island.[1] Despite numerous sources that disproved Briggs's map, mapmakers persisted in retaining California as an island. An error that had almost no basis in fact entered maps of North America shortly after the Pilgrims landed at Plymouth Rock. It persisted on European maps until almost the eve of the American Revolution, despite repeated attempts to correct it. Resistance runs deep whether it is a geophysical map or a mental one!

Why did it take so long to correct such an obvious error in North American mapmaking? Once the error existed on a map, new information was filtered to fit with what the existing map suggested: that California was an island. We constantly do the same thing with our mental maps. We resist changing our mental maps and internal rules of the road by filtering out information and experiences that do not fit. Contradictory information is discounted or ignored.

Sitting in the back of my classroom is a man about fifty years old. He is thinking about a career change and has enrolled in my workshop on spiritual gifts and career development. He has had nearly seven different occupations in every region of the country since graduating from high school but has found no satisfaction in any of them. He is obviously bright and perceptive.

When we review his assessment surveys, he argues with the results. He discounts what they say about his gifts and talents. He insists that his real abilities and interests lie in the occupations he has been pursuing. No matter how long we talk, he cannot entertain alternative possibilities. He has a mental map of who he is and what jobs he should have. He is too certain of his own taken-for-granted mental model to question contradictory information.

We cannot help people grow in love of God and neighbor unless we understand this simple insight from the new science of the brain: We all have mental maps and we resist changing them. Resistance is not a matter of logic and reason. It is an emotional or even spiritual dynamic.

Christian educators have often created classroom environments and group settings that are ideal for assimilative learning. They have multiple tools and strategies that work when learners are adding more detail or facts to what they already know. They have frequently tried to foster transformative learning with these same tools, strategies, and settings. But transformative learning requires different strategies. You cannot cultivate transformative learning with tools designed for assimilation. Accommodation or the restructuring of our mental maps requires a completely different set of strategies that take into consideration the emotional dynamics of resistance.

Fitting the Methods to the Goals

Leaders often take it personally when resistance surfaces in a Sunday school class or a small group. They feel the group is rejecting them. But only rarely is resistance really about the teacher or the leader. Group members are resisting accommodative learning. They are resisting the loss of something important to them. They are resisting the unknown.

Leaders need to see resistance as a sign that they are doing a good job of teaching. If teachers are not encountering some resistance, they are probably not challenging learners to open themselves to the Spirit's ongoing conversion of their hearts and minds.

Teachers cannot address resistance directly. Direct confrontation will only intensify the emotional anxiety that created resistance in the first place. But they can use strategies that indirectly help learners work through resistance. To best utilize these strategies, Christian educators need to understand the interaction between resistance and subject-matter complexity.

Learners and subject matter can be classified by degree of resistance and complexity [see Figure 6.1]. Effective learning depends upon how educators match their teaching strategies to these two variables.

Figure 6.1: Continuum of Subject-Matter Complexity and Learner Resistance

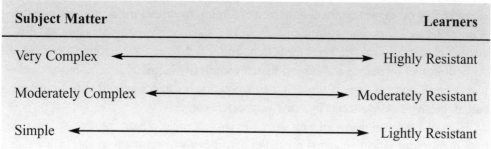

Most church leaders and educators naturally assume low resistance and low complexity. But this is not necessarily the case with either learners or the subject matter. Christian educators need to assess both their subject matter and their students to determine what teaching methods will be most effective in a particular situation. Too often, educators rely on their own favorite teaching strategy, what the lesson plan tells them to do, or what takes the least amount of time and energy to prepare. The new science of the brain suggests that effective teachers adjust their methods to reflect both learner resistance and subject complexity [see Figure 6.2].

Figure 6.2: Possible Teaching Strategies Based on Complexity and Resistance

	Low Complexity	High Complexity
High Resistance	Dialogue	Simulations Role Plays
Low Resistance	Reading Lecture Video	Case Studies Frames Concept Maps

At least three basic principles emerge from Piaget, Kohlberg, and Fowler regarding resistance and subject-matter complexity:

1. As subject matter becomes more complex, the learner's need to interact with it increases.
2. As the learner's resistance to new knowledge or perspectives increases, his or her need to interact with other learners about the new information increases.
3. As both the subject matter's complexity and the learner's resistance increase, the need to interact both with other learners and with the subject matter increases.

Low-involvement methods work well for assimilative learning. Reading and videos are effective in helping learners assimilate more detail into what they already know. These strategies have limited effectiveness as learner resistance and subject-matter complexity increase, however.

Increasing resistance and complexity are signals that accommodative or transformative learning may be happening. Accommodative learning requires a different repertoire of learning technologies than assimilation does. As resistance increases, dialogue and discussion become crucial strategies for helping learners explore their emotional resistance. As both learner resistance and subject-matter complexity increase, simulations and role-plays permit learners to work through their emotional resistance as well as test out new values, behaviors, or concepts in a safe, supportive context.

High-resistance/high-complexity strategies share some common features. All provide opportunities for reflective action related to new ideas, values, or knowledge. They also create environments characterized by hospitality. These environments balance support with challenge. Finally, these environments expose learners to diverse role models. As Kohlberg and Fowler note, observing others who are modeling alternative values or behavior can stretch learners to step forward in their own development.

Keeping in touch with teaching involves keeping in touch with tools and strategies that allow learners to work through their resistance to transformative learning. These strategies neutralize our powerful instinct not to change and grow even when we consciously say we desire growth and transformation.

Dialogue and Discussion

Dialogue and discussion are key strategies for high-resistance situations. Through dialogue, we move from being passive consumers of information to being active contributors in a community of learning. Dialogue cannot be forced or contrived. But it can be cultivated. Christian educators can create the conditions under which it can emerge and flourish. The ability to cultivate a climate of dialogue is one of the Christian educator's most important capacities.

Purposes of Dialogue

Dialogue serves cognitive, emotional, and social purposes. For these reasons, dialogue has tremendous potential for disarming resistance. Some of dialogue's cognitive or intellectual purposes include:

1. exploring a diversity of opinions;
2. discovering and examining diverse perspectives;
3. emphasizing the complexity and ambiguity of issues;
4. recognizing the assumptions underlying habitual thoughts and behaviors;
5. encouraging active listening.

Some of dialogue's emotional goals are:

1. increasing learners' emotional connection to a topic, which is essential for transformative learning;
2. showing that opinions matter.

Dialogue also cultivates some specific social or group outcomes such as:

1. strengthening group identity;
2. encouraging unity amid diversity.

Powerful Questions—The Heart of Dialogue

Powerful questions lie at the heart of transformative learning. Powerful questions challenge our assumptive worlds and mental maps. Powerful questions get a dialogue moving and keep it moving.

Everyone can learn to ask more powerful questions that encourage people to examine and revise their mental maps. Powerful questions are directed toward learning rather than reporting, accommodation rather than assimilation. Almost every Christian educator and leader can learn to ask a wider range of questions. A widely accepted classification of questions was developed by Benjamin Bloom.[2] He categorized questions based on factual knowledge, comprehension, application, analysis, synthesis, and evaluation [see Figure 6.3].

Factual Questions. Factual questions ask learners to recall specific facts or information. Factual questions deal with who, what, where, when, and how. Factual questions are most appropriate when the instructional goal is assimilation rather than accommodation.

Examples of factual questions are:

- Who were the main characters in Jesus' parable of the forgiving father?
- Who did Paul meet with when he came to Jerusalem?
- After Elijah defeated the prophets of Baal on Mt. Carmel, where did he go and who did he meet on the way?

Factual questions are narrowly focused. For this reason, factual questions are useful for moving learners into a topic or subject. They cannot, however, sustain or deepen a conversation.

Factual questions are the basic building blocks for the other levels of questioning. Factual questions are easy to formulate. Unfortunately, the ease with which leaders can pose such questions results in their overuse. Based on my personal observations, I would say factual questions constitute nearly half of all the questions that the average teacher asks. Over-reliance on factual questions will sabotage dialogue before it begins.

Comprehension Questions. Comprehension questions invite participants to organize and select facts or ideas. They also ask learners to relate one idea to another. In the process, learners begin to explore how new information fits with existing mental maps. Comprehension questions require group members to paraphrase or summarize new information in their own words, thus forming mental connections.

Type of Question	Description	Example
Factual Knowledge	Asks for facts or information specific to the topic	Who are the main characters in Jesus' parable of the forgiving father?
Comprehension	Asks about the meaning of the topic or content Asks learners to summarize or paraphrase content Asks learners to explain relationships between ideas or people	What does it mean for the oldest son to have stayed at home with the father?
Application	Asks learners to demonstrate the relevance or applicability of the content	In what ways have we been like the older brother in this parable?
Analysis	Asks learners to analyze the content by taking it apart and reconstructing it in new terms	What interactions and interconnections do you see between the younger and the older brother in this parable?
Synthesis	Asks learners to form new ideas using connections between this content and previous knowledge or experience	What other parables or biblical stories make the same point as this parable?
Evaluation	Asks learners to evaluate or make judgments about the content	How would you evaluate the effectiveness of this parable in making Jesus' point about God's grace?

Some comprehension questions are:

- What is the significance of Luke writing that the angels appeared to shepherds near Bethlehem?
- What meaning do you see in having the older son stay at home in the parable of the forgiving father?

Questions of Application. Questions of application challenge learners to apply what they are learning to specific situations in their own lives. Like comprehension questions, these questions invite learners to connect new knowledge with something they already know. Application questions allow learners to explore how new subject matter fits with previous experience and knowledge.

Examples of application questions are:

- In what ways is Isaiah's vision in Chapter 6 like the parts of our worship service?
- What are some ways we have been like the older brother in this parable?
- What does the process of decision-making at the Jerusalem Council (Acts 15) say to us about how we make decisions in the church?

Analytic Questions. Analytic questions build on the earlier levels. Once learners have reflected on basic facts and comprehended the topic, they can begin to draw their own conclusions.

Learners analyze what this new knowledge means. Analytic questions engage the learner actively in thinking and reflecting. Learners must take apart and reconstruct newly presented information in light of what they already know. With sensitive and thoughtful follow-up, these questions help learners identify the underlying mental maps framing their thinking. These questions require much effort and care to formulate.

- What are the main scenes in Jesus' parable of the forgiving father and what is the flow from one to the next?
- How do the major leadership roles in the early church according to Acts 6 relate organizationally and ethnically?

Analytic questions also require more time to answer than other types of questions. While group members may answer a factual question almost as soon as the facilitator asks it, an analytic question may be followed by a long pause or silence. Group leaders need to allow learners time to formulate their responses to an analytic question and not rush to the next question or jump in with their own answer. Leaders serve dialogue best by providing group members with the time and space to let an analytic question do its work.

Synthesizing Questions. Synthesizing questions require group members to come up with their own answers. They must be able to draw upon what they already know and put together a novel or new response. Synthesizing questions invite learners to examine how new information relates to what they already know. How can it shift or transform their present mental maps or their taken-for-granted rules of the road? How will it fit or not fit?

Synthesizing questions are open-ended and have no correct answer.

- In what other parables or biblical stories do we find the same message about how God treats us that we find in the parable of the forgiving father?
- What is similar about these stories of God calling people to be prophets?
- What connections do you see between Matthew's nativity story and stories in Genesis about Joseph in Egypt?

These questions work only in groups characterized by mutual respect, listening, and hospitality. Without these qualities, synthesizing questions lose much of their impact. Group members will not reconstruct knowledge into a new whole if they fear they will be made wrong by the leader or other group members.

Evaluative Questions. Evaluative questions invite learners to make a value judgment about something.

- What do you personally think about the message of forgiveness in Jesus' parable of the forgiving father?
- What is your personal opinion of Amos' condemnation of Israel's worship as noisy assemblies that God despises?
- How would you evaluate the success of Paul's preaching in Athens?

For these questions to work effectively, facilitators must ask learners to express both their value judgment and the criteria upon which they have reached their conclusion. Too often class leaders ask for a value judgment and stop. They do not proceed to the more critical task of asking learners to explicate the criteria behind their judgment. Surfacing this underlying assumptive framework of values creates the possibility of examining and changing one's current mental map. So long as this internal framework is assumed and hidden, learners cannot question it or alter it. They remain prisoners to unexamined assumptions.

A supportive, caring group climate is essential for asking evaluative questions. Group members will not risk answering these questions if they fear being judged or embarrassed.

These questions also cannot be answered in a nanosecond. Christian educators and leaders need to allow some silence in which participants inwardly formulate their responses. Too often leaders underutilize these questions because they are uncomfortable with the silence or lack of immediate response. They therefore quickly revert to factual or comprehension questions.

Having a clear typology of questions enables teachers and group leaders to ask the right question at the right time. Sunday school teachers and Bible class leaders sometimes want to jump immediately to higher-order questions. These questions are often met by silence and blank looks. Learners need time to move into the material and open up their own thinking. Jumping too quickly to complex evaluative or synthetic questions short-circuits this process. Effective teachers and leaders instead sequence their questions, beginning with factual or comprehension questions and then moving toward ones that require higher-order thinking [see Figure 6.4].

Others undermine discussion by asking only factual questions. They remain stuck at the lower end of Bloom's typology. In some classes, half of all questions rehearse factual information. The result is a flat, dull conversation. We skim along the surface of our thoughts, never diving deeper. Bible teachers and group leaders can make their classrooms sparkle when they liberally sprinkle all six types of questions into their lesson plans.

Figure 6.4: Sequencing Questions to Move a Dialogue Forward

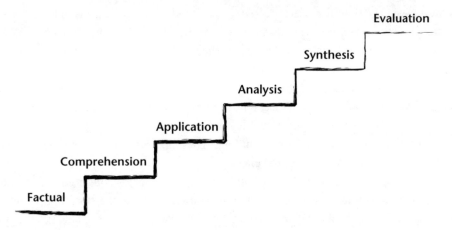

Asking the Right Questions

The ability of dialogue to expose and transform learners' mental maps will depend largely on the quality of questions Christian educators ask. Not all questions are created equal. Some questions create a free and hospitable space for dialogue. Other questions shut down conversation and close up participants.

Ask "What," Not "Why." My sons played soccer when they were younger. One year they had a terrific coach who called forth the best in them. This coach had a knack for asking the right question in the right way.

Other coaches would shout, "Are you watching the ball?" or "Why don't you keep your eye on the ball?" These questions made my sons defensive. Even if they were not watching the ball, they would say that they were. Once they became defensive, it was difficult for them to listen to the coach's suggestions.

The coach who knew how to ask the right questions asked completely different questions. She would say, "What way was the ball spinning as it came to you?" Or: "How far were you from the ball when you first moved into a position to kick it?" Her questions almost compelled them to look at the ball. How else could they answer which way it was spinning? Her questions heightened their awareness of their own experience. The answers she sought were always descriptive, not judgmental. This coach's questions prompted Robert and Jonathan to use higher-order skills of analysis. They encouraged reflective practice.

Good questions heighten self-awareness and focus attention. They encourage exploration and reflection. Such questions usually begin with *What.* Powerful questions seldom begin with *Why. Why* questions almost automatically make people defensive. They shut people down. A question that begins with *Why* implies criticism. *Why* questions only increase resistance. They send people to a place of defensive self-justification rather than to curious self-exploration. Such questions are deadly for dialogue. They erect a huge stop sign in the middle of the conversation.

How questions can also heighten resistance. They send people into analysis rather than self-awareness. *How* questions send people to their heads. But resistance is in the emotions. To deal with resistance, people need to get out of their heads and into their emotions. If the goal of dialogue is to help people surface their assumptive maps and mental rules of the road, then facilitators will only occasionally ask *How* questions.

Ask Open-Ended Questions. Effective questions are usually open-ended. They do not require a "yes" or "no" answer. Closed-ended questions, on the other hand, reflect the teacher's unconscious attempt to control learners' responses. Closed-ended questions do not encourage higher-order, reflective thinking. These questions may work great in the courtroom. But they are deadly in the classroom.

Avoid Asking Questions That Make You Look Smart. Teachers and group leaders can stop dialogue in its tracks by asking leading questions. Leading questions imply there is one right answer. Leading questions leave little room for exploration. They hint that the desired answer is built into the question itself. Participants intuitively recognize a leading question. They are left feeling manipulated. Leading questions shatter a group's climate of trust and openness. They deprive members of psychological safety.

Powerful questions are different from smart questions. Powerful questions, in fact, often seem like dumb questions. Most of us have trained ourselves to look smart, particularly if we are the teacher, leader, or facilitator. We think we should ask smart questions. We think that if we can ask a really brilliant question, the whole group will notice how smart we are. But smart questions seldom move dialogue forward. They focus the attention on us, not the shared meaning that group members are building in the midst of their conversation.

One way to avoid asking smart questions is to ask short questions. If my question is longer than five to seven words, it is too long. Listeners get lost in a long question. They will hear my own assumptions rather than the question. If I ask a brief question, I have less time to erect a frame of my own beliefs, values, or mental models around it. The shorter and simpler my question, the more power it has to evoke curiosity, stimulate self-awareness, and focus the learner's attention.

Use Silence to Make Your Questions More Powerful. Expect silence after you ask a powerful question. These questions need time to land. Learners will have a factual answer on the tip of their tongues. But they must go inside themselves to answer a truly powerful question.

As teachers and group leaders, we are sometimes uncomfortable with silence. We are tempted to blurt out another question or to rephrase the same question in another way. Blurting out a different question or rephrasing the same question actually serves to confuse listeners. It muddies the waters. "What is being asked?" they wonder, "The first question or this one? Are they different or the same?" If you tape record yourself or listen carefully to your teaching, you will probably discover that you repeat a question or rephrase it more often than you think. Simply changing this behavior will significantly improve your ability to ask powerful questions.

We often interpret a group's silence as confusion about the meaning of the question, not as an introspective moment of self-awareness. Effective Sunday school teachers and group leaders learn to be comfortable with silence. One useful technique is to ask a question, then count silently to ten before saying another word. Counting silently to ten serves as a brake on our tendency to ask another question or rephrase our original question. It creates a space where a question, if powerful, can land with listeners.

Sometimes, if I have counted to ten and no one is speaking, I may say something like: "I'm not sure how to interpret the silence. What does our silence mean? It could be you are still thinking. Or it might mean my question wasn't clear. If it's how I asked the question, could someone try to rephrase it?"

Sometimes the silence means that participants are reluctant to speak in a large group for fear of embarrassing themselves. So I might ask everyone to turn to a neighbor and respond to the question. Once people have opened up on a one-to-one basis, they may feel freer speaking to the whole class.

Acknowledge Every Answer. Finally, be sure to affirm learners when they respond to a question regardless of the quality or correctness of their answer. Learners need feedback. If someone answers your question and you provide no response, the whole group will quickly learn that no answers are really expected or wanted. Or they will learn that they should only speak if they are certain they have the "right" answer. The most effective technique is to ask a question, wait for someone to answer, respond specifically to that answer, and then pose another question.

Planning for Dialogue

In addition to asking powerful questions, the most important decision in planning a dialogue is "What kind of dialogue do we want to have?" Church educators can design three different types of dialogues: focused, open-ended, or mixed. A focused dialogue involves covering a clearly defined topic and moving through a series of planned steps. An open-ended dialogue represents the other end of the continuum. The leader poses an initial question or topic and then allows the group to go wherever it wishes. A mixed dialogue includes both focused and open-ended components. Each type requires different preparation and preplanning.

Planning a focused dialogue involves a series of intentional steps [see Figure 6.5]. The group leader or facilitator first reads through the lesson or curriculum unit and makes an outline of the material. Next, major points in the lesson's readings are translated into a question or questions. Each question or subquestion corresponds to the outline's sections and subsections. These questions and subquestions then guide the flow of the dialogue. The teacher or group leader will be sure to ask various types of questions—from factual to application to evaluative ones. Under each type of question, there may be several subquestions that help deepen the dialogue.

Designing a focused dialogue works well for Sunday school teachers and group leaders who like structure and some element of predictability in their classroom. They know where they begin and where they will end. They have a full repertoire of questions they can pose and are confident they will not be left unsure what to ask.

Skillful teachers can lead a focused dialogue without seeming controlling or predictable. They can use learners' comments as a springboard for their next question. Even though this type of conversation is carefully designed, it can seem spontaneous and natural.

An open-ended dialogue, on the other hand, does not try to direct the flow of conversation. At first glance, it might seem like an open-ended dialogue would require less planning than a focused one. Nothing could be further from the truth. Open-ended dialogue may, in fact, require more planning and forethought [see Figure 6.6].

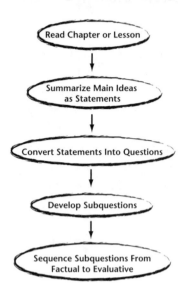

Figure 6.6: Planning an Open-Ended Dialogue

Planning for an open-ended dialogue begins exactly like planning for a focused dialogue. The teacher or group leader reads the chapter or lesson and summarizes its main ideas. He or she then develops an outline of the main points. Rather than convert this outline into a sequence of well-designed questions that move through the topic, however, the instructor brainstorms all the possible connections between these ideas and other experiences, ideas, beliefs, or behaviors. Some teachers and group leaders find it helpful to visualize learners in the group and imagine what ideas or concepts will be important to them and why.

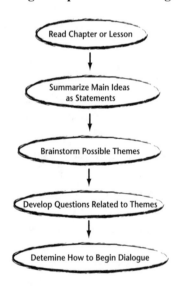

The facilitator may even create a mind map or concept map illustrating all these connections. This visual display can help the facilitator develop possible questions to begin the dialogue and serve as a prompt for further discussion during the dialogue.

Next, the teacher or group leader determines how to begin the dialogue. Some typical possibilities are:

1. Personally share a situation in your own life that connects to the reading and then ask others if they have had a similar experience.
2. Invite learners to recall events in their lives that connect with this lesson.

3. Ask learners to list all the key themes or ideas they found in the lesson and write them on a dry-erase board or newsprint. Then ask them to choose which topic they want to explore.
4. Introduce some dissonance by presenting facts or opinions that contradict or subvert the lesson. Then invite students to share their reactions.

Mixed dialogues include elements from both focused and open-ended dialogue. Most learning settings in the church are more likely to involve mixed dialogue. Some of the class session is focused on the lesson or reading. At other times, the group engages in open-ended sharing. Teachers planning for mixed dialogue should decide whether they believe the session will lean more toward focused dialogue or open-ended conversation. They then plan according to the general direction they anticipate the session will go.

Beginning a Dialogue

Starting a dialogue can produce a few awkward moments. The teacher or leader may be greeted by uncomfortable silence. Or she may find herself trying to coax and cajole a few participants into speaking.

Establish Ground Rules or Norms. Beginning a dialogue session is easier when participants have agreed upon ground rules that help insure a hospitable climate [see Figure 6.7]. These ground rules or behavioral covenants include agreements to tell the truth as each person knows it, to limit the time any single individual may speak, or to seek to understand another's perspective rather than change or alter how they think.

Ground rules are not an end in themselves. They help create a safe container for conversation and dialogue. Without them, learners may not know what they may safely communicate. They may not know what behaviors or statements are out-of-bounds in this setting. In order to overcome resistance to learning, groups need norms that engender as much psychological safety as possible.

Figure 6.7: Suggested Ground Rules

We will
1. account for our absences so the group does not wait on us;
2. keep our focus on the topic we are discussing;
3. avoid side conversations and whispering;
4. describe behaviors and specific actions, not character or motivation;
5. use examples and specifics rather than speak in generalities;
6. explain the reasoning behind our statements and opinions;
7. support each other's spiritual growth;
8. begin and end with prayer or worship;
9. seek to understand others' viewpoints rather than criticize or convert them.

Model How to Be a Partner in Dialogue. If the leader does not model effective listening, participants will not listen to each other. If the leader models sarcasm or being judgmental, group members will quickly judge and criticize each other. Teachers and group leaders who want to foster powerful learning will model the skills and habits that encourage dialogue.

Some possible behaviors to model are:

1. Stop talking. After you ask a question, do not answer it yourself. Participants will learn that they can outwait you with their silence. They will learn that you already know what the "right" answer is, so they do not need to bother to share their opinions.

2. Look, act, and be interested in what others say. If you are shuffling through your notes, looking out the window, whispering to someone else while participants are talking, then group members will learn that they do not need to pay attention to any opinion other than their own.

3. Do not interrupt a speaker.

4. Enter into another participant's viewpoint and try genuinely to understand what he or she is saying. Your genuine interest will model empathy and nonjudgmental listening for the whole group.

5. Resist the temptation to make critical or evaluative comments immediately after someone speaks. As the dialogue moves forward, the time will come for deeper exploration and critical thinking.

6. Be careful how you use humor. Some participants may experience your comments as put-downs or implicit criticism. People will not speak if they think they will become the object of ridicule or criticism.

7. Practice active listening in which you summarize or paraphrase what others have said before responding to them.

8. Express appreciation and enthusiasm when someone introduces a new perspective or takes a risk in what they share.

9. Stop talking. Do not use someone's comment as the springboard for a mini-lecture. If you want to give a lecture or make a presentation, then design the class session around that task. Do not bill a lecture class as a dialogue session.

Start Slow and Build. In general, starting slowly with factual questions is the best approach. Factual questions are the easiest for participants to answer and involve the least risk. Teachers and group leaders can build gradually toward higher-order questions. Such questions give learners the confidence to invest themselves in the conversation.

Factual questions also construct a common framework of information. If the leader asks a series of factual questions about Elijah's encounter with the widow of Zarephath, everyone in the group can rehearse and recall the basic flow of the story. These questions establish a shared understanding upon which the group can build as the dialogue progresses.

Some teachers mistakenly believe they can skip over factual or comprehension questions and move directly to questions of evaluation or synthesis. When group leaders move immediately to these higher-order questions, learners may feel overwhelmed or ill-prepared to answer. Conversely, some teachers continue asking factual questions long after they are productive. Once learners have rehearsed the facts and built a common framework of meaning, they quickly lose interest if the teacher continues posing factual questions.

During this stage, it is particularly important for the teacher to acknowledge every response, even those which are not exactly correct or productive. Acknowledging every response signals to the class that participation is valued and will not be met with criticism, judgment, or sarcasm.

Keeping Dialogue Alive

Once the ball is rolling, how do you keep it moving? Getting a classroom conversation started is no assurance that it will blossom and thrive. After some initial remarks, it may sputter out or fizzle. Resistance to examining one's assumptions can be crafty and deeply engrained. So what can a teacher or group leader do?

First, teachers and group leaders can avoid the temptation to inject a mini-lecture into the give-and-take of dialogue. Learners may respond by treating the teacher as the resident expert whose opinion counts for more than their own. So they settle back into silence.

Second, teachers can affirm every response. One mistake leaders often make is asking questions and then, after learners give a verbal response, failing to give any feedback. The participant's remarks fall like a plop in the middle of the room. If group leaders respond to every comment and give feedback early in the class session, participants will learn that their viewpoints matter and they will be acknowledged. Even if the answer is inadequate or incorrect, the teacher can at least affirm the student for taking the risk of responding.

Third, if the conversation is lagging, teachers can introduce new energy by breaking the class into pairs or triads for discussion. Another possible strategy involves asking students to generate as many responses as possible: "Quick, let's brainstorm how many ways the prodigal son's older brother might have responded." Such instructions invite learners to pick up the pace of the conversation. Conversely, group leaders can slow down a conversation so that everyone goes deeper. "Let's allow that statement to really sink in for a minute before we respond. Take a moment to think about how you want to respond to Patty's remarks."

Fourth, leaders can redirect the conversation to a more specific or more abstract level. Such a shift can alter the conversation's pace and depth. If the group is dealing in generalities and abstractions, the teacher can say: "Let's give some specific examples of where Paul's teaching on spiritual gifts comes alive in our own congregation." If the group is being too concrete and literal, the teacher might ask, "Let's see if there are some generalizations we can take from the examples we have been giving."

Ending Dialogue

Dialogues conclude even when issues are not settled and thoughts are not shared. The Sunday school bell rings. Children or parents begin to peer through the door or knock.

People get up to join the choir or prepare to usher. Teachers and group leaders need to plan how they will bring the session to a close. A sense of closure is important for participants. Even though the discussion may not be finished, learners need to feel they have reached completion for this time and place.

Leaders therefore need to plan how and when they will bring closure to a dialogue. Usually at least seven to ten minutes should be left free at the end of the class for closure activities. One way to conclude a session is for the teacher or group leader to offer a summary of how the dialogue has evolved and some of its key points. This is helpful especially to those participants who dislike discussion or dialogue formats, complaining that they are only "pooling our ignorance." Another option is to have each learner share one important understanding or insight he or she has gained.

However the leader chooses to conclude a session, it is important that participants feel closure has been reached. Nothing is worse than participants exiting the room while others are in midsentence. No one likes leaving with the feeling that everything has been left "up in the air."

Dialogue is a powerful tool for helping learners examine their assumptions and alter their mental maps. Your goals as a Christian educator include more than helping learners add detail to their existing mental maps. Teachers and small-group leaders have a responsibility for encouraging learners to examine their fundamental assumptions so they do not conform to this world but are transformed by the renewing of their minds through the living Word of God, Jesus Christ. Dialogue is an essential practice for such transformative or accommodative learning.

Resistance and Experiential Learning

When subject matter is complex and learner resistance is high, Christian educators and leaders may wish to use more experiential methods. Experiential methods include a variety of simulation tools such as roleplays and simulation exercises. These strategies promote intense involvement both with the subject matter and with other participants.

Advantages and Disadvantages of Simulation Tools

Simulation tools have several advantages. They allow learners to process new knowledge actively rather than simply receive it passively. Active processing is especially critical when both learner resistance and subject-matter complexity are high. Since roleplays are usually based on real-life situations, participants are able to make mental or neural connections that foster later recall and usage. In addition, people are usually more receptive to new ideas or behaviors when they are actively involved in the processing of learning and feel a greater sense of control over it.

Roleplays, case studies, critical incidents, and other types of simulations also have some disadvantages. Learners may generalize inappropriately. They may apply to every relationship a new behavior they learned in a single simulation. Sometimes the roleplay will be overly complicated and cause learners to lose confidence in themselves when they cannot perform it successfully.

Roleplay also depends heavily upon the facilitation skills of the group leader or teacher. The quality of participants' learning often hinges on the facilitator's ability to pose effective questions, to provide short and clear instructions, and to guide discovery learning. Teachers must be able to move from disseminating information to facilitating learning. Without adequate training and experience, some Sunday school teachers and small-group leaders may have difficulty making this transition.

Despite these disadvantages, simulations are extremely powerful learning tools. They provide a unique opportunity for learner ownership of new knowledge, values, and behavior.

Designing and Using Roleplays in Christian Education

Human beings are complex. We think, feel, and act all at the same time. While these systems are interconnected in the human brain, they are not always in sync with one another. We can sometimes think one thing, do another, and feel a third.

Stan often speaks about servant leadership. He opens his committee meetings with devotions that call attention to this theme. Although his espoused theory is servant leadership, Stan's actual theory-in-action is quite autocratic. Stan's thinking, feeling, and acting are not congruent.

The most effective way to reach Stan is to communicate with him on all levels: thinking, feeling, and acting. Otherwise, Stan's deeply engrained habits of thought and action will powerfully resist new insights. Roleplaying is designed to breach these defenses. Roleplaying is effective precisely because it communicates with the totality of who we are as thinking, feeling, and acting human beings. For these reasons, it is particularly useful when resistance to learning is high and the topic is complex or ambiguous.

Roleplay engages people in actual behaviors. In a roleplay, no separation exists between words, thoughts, and actions. A roleplay allows learners to participate actively through exploring, experimenting, and actually trying out new behaviors and responses in a safe setting.

A time-tested method of experiential learning is coaching or apprenticeship. Our sons learn soccer plays and rules from a guidebook. But their coaches also place them in actual practice situations where they can work with them to identify mistakes and rehearse alternative responses. Roleplay allows this same opportunity to surface assumptive worlds and to receive coaching on alternative mental models in a safe, hospitable setting.

Components of a Roleplay. Roleplays include at least six basic steps: climate-setting, action, sharing, processing, generalization, and application [see Figure 6.8].

Climate-setting is absolutely crucial for a roleplay. The development of an open, non-judgmental climate occurs before meaningful involvement and learning can happen. Climate-setting involves establishing ground rules for participation that allow learners to feel safe and free. Climate-setting also includes providing learners with the basic facts, information, or concepts they need to participate.

Figure 6.8: Design Steps for Roleplay

Climate-Setting ➤ Action ➤ Sharing ➤ Processing ➤ Generalization ➤ Application

Step	Design Task
Climate-Setting	Establish ground rules: • climate of support • nonjudgmental responses • open participation
Action	Design and implement roleplay: • set context for scenario • provide short, clear instructions • monitor participation
Sharing	Focus on communicating observations and feelings. Do not process the meaning of the experience.
Processing	Process the meaning of the experience: significance, insights, interconnections.
Generalization	Generalize from these meanings and insights to other settings or situations. How does this experience fit in with what I already know or believe? How does it change what I know or believe?
Application	Explore how to apply these generalizations in specific life situations of the participants. Develop action steps.

Action is the core of the roleplay process. Learners actually engage in playing out a particular situation or behavior.

During a time of sharing and processing, learners process their experience through reflection and analysis. They debrief the experience and prepare for new action.

Finally, learners extract general principles from the roleplay that they can apply to other settings and situations. During the generalization and application phases, learners adapt their mental maps to incorporate these new experiences and insights.

Types of Roleplays. Christian educators may use at least two types of roleplays, structured and unstructured. Structured roleplays involve considerable preplanning. The goals or objectives are predetermined. Prepared scripts that describe the situation and players are given to participants. The action is carefully orchestrated. Unstructured, or developmental, roleplays emerge more spontaneously and the action develops rather than being predetermined.

Christian educators are sometimes supplied with structured roleplays. Their curriculum may furnish scripts and possible roles. In other cases, a teacher or group leader may determine that a spontaneous or unstructured roleplay may be an effective way to address resistance and deepen learning.

Lights! Camera! Action! If a Sunday school teacher or small-group leader wishes to use a roleplay, some suggested steps are:

1. Establish the ground rules for a nonevaluative, nonthreatening climate. Don't just jump in by asking for volunteers, passing out scripts, and starting. Set the stage properly. Teachers can carefully phrase their instructions to avoid creating the wrong climate. "Let's look at three or four possible ways a Christian might use Matthew 18 to deal with conflict" has a different impact from saying, "Let's see how well someone can follow Matthew's instructions on handling conflict."

2. Ask for volunteers. Do not force people to participate in a roleplay. Some people are reluctant to appear before a group, especially if they fear they might be asked to do or say something embarrassing.

3. Assign participants to roles other than their normal church office or function. If a Sunday school teacher is describing a difficult student, give him the role of being a student—not the teacher. Ask the pastor to play the role of the hospital patient, not the visiting pastor. Don't ask the council chair to play the chairperson's role. Roleplaying gets people out of their usual roles and perspectives. It also lessens their anxiety that they will be judged on the basis of their performance.

4. Have the group propose several approaches rather than asking players to demonstrate their own approach. When an individual is asked to demonstrate how they personally would respond, evaluation or judgment can enter into the process. To avoid this, the facilitator can ask group members to describe several possible ways the players might speak or act. The person in the role then follows the group's lead on what should be done. Thus, the person is not following a personal preference but experimenting with approaches the group has generated. This approach diminishes the risk that feedback will be personalized.

5. Use role rotation. Rather than having only one person play the key role in the scene, rotate other group members through this role. This practice avoids the danger that everyone will overfocus on a single individual's skill, knowledge, or competency. Remember, the goal of roleplay is group learning, not individual evaluation. In setting up the roleplay, a good facilitator says something like, "Now, it is important that everyone listen carefully to what Analiese is saying because every two or three minutes I will ask someone to step into Analiese's role. You will be expected to pick up right where she left off."

6. Maximize connections between players and observers. Roleplays are effective when observers feel they are represented by those in the roleplay. Roleplay loses its effectiveness when observers feel they are separate from the players and somehow sitting in judgment on them or evaluating them. Facilitators can strengthen this con-

nection by carefully establishing the original scene and the context for learning. They can also reinforce it by interventions during the roleplay. For example, the facilitator might stop the action and ask, "Can anyone suggest something Analiese might try to get Enrique's attention?" or "What do you think Enrique might do next?" Role rotations also serve to keep the observers connected to the action.

Sharing. Immediately after the roleplay, everyone needs an opportunity to talk about their responses and reactions to the experience. This conversation mostly focuses on emotions and feelings, although some conceptual insights may also surface. This talking about emotions is important. It is where resistance may begin to soften and dissipate.

During the talking phase, the facilitator does not comment on the process or meaning of the roleplay. Instead, the focus is on the sharing of feelings and observations. As a facilitator, I usually ask for impressions, feelings, or specific observations. I may ask, "At what point did you feel most involved in this roleplay? And what was the source of your involvement?" or "Where did you see yourself in this experience?" I might also pose the question, "What did you personally feel when your partner said ... ?"

Processing. "Experience is the best teacher," we often say. Yet people do not always learn from experience. They may learn nothing. Or they may learn the wrong thing. Processing is essential if we are to learn from our experience. Some teachers mistakenly believe that a roleplay stands on its own. They simply assign roles, do the exercise, and then move to the next item in their lesson plan. When this happens, learners are deprived of important learning. The goal of processing is new understanding. If sharing serves to address learner resistance, processing is where subject-matter complexity is made more manageable. As common themes emerge, they can be captured on newsprint or a dry-erase board.

Because we are so prone to criticize, judge, and evaluate—especially in classroom settings—the facilitator must emphasize that processing is about providing new insights, opportunities, and support for everyone. It is not about evaluating players' performances.

Generalization. Like dialogue, roleplays need some sense of closure and completion. This is the most important phase in the whole process. When omitted, learners may feel the class session was superficial or a waste of time. Participants have been through a series of experiences that suggest possible changes in their thinking, acting, valuing, or perceiving. Now is their opportunity to reflect concretely on these possibilities. They connect these insights back to the lesson's original content or subject matter.

Application. The final stage of roleplay poses the question "Now what?" The participants need an opportunity to reflect on concrete actions they might take in light of these experiences. How can they apply what they learned from the roleplay? Learners may generalize about concepts or principles rather than specific actions. Depending upon the size of the group, participants may be broken into smaller buzz groups where they can talk about how to apply what they have learned.

CONCLUSION

Because roleplays and other simulation techniques involve people emotionally as well as cognitively, they provide a powerful container where participants can work through their resistance and engage in transformative or accommodative learning. Dialogue, roleplay, and simulation all offer ways to incorporate basic principles that Kohlberg and Fowler contribute to Christian faith formation. These teaching strategies combine high challenge with high support. They create settings in which learners are stretched beyond their current assumptive worlds through a dialogic and experiential encounter with people who may hold very different perspectives or embody very different faith and moral outlooks. These strategies challenge our ever-active brains to seek new patterns of meaning and coherence.

Deepening Your Learning

1. Select a New Testament parable or an Old Testament story. Design a question sequence for an adult Bible study. Be sure to ask all six levels of questions. Notice your own thought process as you do this.

2. If you have the opportunity to lead an adult Bible study, take your design and actually use it with your group. Notice the group's responses. What do you learn about asking powerful questions?

3. Practice asking short questions this week. Try to ask questions that are only five to seven words long. Observe your thoughts and feelings. Notice how others respond to your questions. What do you learn about asking questions? How can this experience make you a better Christian educator?

4. Notice at least twenty times this week when you experience resistance to something. Keep a journal or make notes on these experiences. What provoked resistance? What did your emotional resistance feel like? What did you do with your resistance? Then reflect on your experiences and ask what they suggest about dealing with resistance as a Christian educator or church leader.

5. Have someone observe you teach and then give you feedback. Ask them to count all the times you (a) rephrase a question before someone has an opportunity to answer; (b) answer your own questions before someone responds; (c) fail to acknowledge a response; or (d) ask "Why" questions. What can you learn from this feedback to become a more effective Christian educator?

ENDNOTES

1 One account of the story of Briggs's map can be found in *A Failure of Nerve: Leadership in the Age of the Quick Fix,* by Edwin H. Friedman (The Edwin Friedman Estate/Trust, 1999), pages 56-58.

2 See *Taxonomy of Educational Objectives: The Classification of Educational Goals,* edited by Benjamin S. Bloom (David McKay Company, 1956).

CHAPTER SEVEN

Doers of the Word and Not Hearers Only

Linking Faith and Faithfulness

S imulations and roleplays are powerful learning tools precisely because they invite us to reflect critically on our experiences. Such critical reflection is not limited to Sunday school classrooms or mid-week Bible studies, however. Congregational life as a whole provides almost unlimited opportunities for discovery learning through critical reflection on experiences in ministry.

Life in Christian community is about following Jesus. Following Jesus is not neatly divided into a two-step sequence in which we first learn about discipleship and then later practice acts of discipleship. When Jesus calls Peter, James, and John, he does not sit them down in a classroom and give them fifty-five hours of instruction before asking them to follow him. They learn to become his disciples as they practice discipleship. Learning is not preparatory to life. It is life.

Weaving a Spider Web of Learning Opportunities

We do not first learn about Christian discipleship in a classroom or Bible study group and only afterward engage in ministry. Instead, we are shaped for ministry through ministry. Effective Christian discipleship links faith with faithfulness, action with reflection. We learn to be followers of Jesus as we concretely follow him in ministry and service. As we reflect on our experiences of following Jesus, we deepen our understanding of what it means to be his disciples.

Unfortunately, congregations sometimes encourage people to think about their faith in one setting (a classroom) and apply it in another (a meeting, a neighborhood, a workplace). Church meetings are places where we plan *for* the church without ever expecting to *be* the church. Yet every congregational setting offers an opportunity to stop automatically processing our experiences, to reflect on our assumptions, and to envision alternative ways of being, knowing, or doing that embody more faithfully the good news of Jesus Christ.

Everything the church does provides people with opportunities to name their experiences, reflect upon their assumptive frameworks, and make choices about how to live as God's covenant people. The church does not *have* an educational program. It *is* an educational program. God is not limited to a classroom or Bible study. God stands at the door of everyday experience and knocks, hoping we will open the doors of perception and reflect on God's presence, purpose, and power in our lives.

Planning for Formal and Informal Learning

Planning for Christian education extends beyond the Sunday school, midweek enrichment programs, and Bible studies. Effective Christian educators weave a spider web of teaching and learning across the whole congregation and its ministries. They find partners in learning everywhere within the congregation.

The most important mental map for Christian educators to challenge is the one that designates a specific hour on Sunday morning as the primary hour for Christian teaching and learning. The most critical change in their own mental maps entails a shift from seeing Christians as passive consumers of religious information to seeing them as a community of learners who critically examine and transform their assumptive worlds in light of an ongoing encounter with Jesus Christ.

Church members need settings for formal instruction. But Christians also need informal learning opportunities where they can engage in reflection-in-action. While congregations often give careful thought and resources to the first setting, they just as frequently overlook the critical importance of the latter.

The ministry of the laity—both inside the church and in the world—represents a rich resource for reflection-in-action. Consistent participation in action-reflection experiences keeps groups of Christians from becoming self-absorbed communities, sealed off from real life and its complexities. So how can church educators and leaders encourage the informal learning that occurs through reflection-in-action?

Whenever individuals or groups solve problems, make decisions, engage in ministry, or plan for the future, they are learning. Assumptive worlds are revealed, challenged, and critiqued. Complex thinking is fostered. New experiences are transformed into a deposit of remembered meaning. Mental models are restructured. Unspoken rules of the road are transformed. In almost every church gathering, church leaders are shaping and reshaping meaning in a community of learners who seek to practice the faith in obedience to God's Word.

Christian educators and leaders have a responsibility to cultivate and encourage thoughtful Christian reflection-in-action in every church committee, board, council, and small group.

CRITICAL THINKING CHALLENGES A STANCE OF CERTITUDE

Faith formation in both formal and informal learning settings occurs when people move beyond their certitudes and uncover the fundamental assumptive frameworks that limit their ability to love, know, and serve God. So long as people are certain that their present mental maps are absolutely correct, they are not open to the Spirit's guidance.

From a place of certitude, we are unable and unwilling to question our mental maps and assumed rules of the road. Certitude absolutizes our taken-for-granted assumptions. Certitude reduces faith to ideology. The gospels provide many examples of the cost exacted by religious certitude. Jesus' opponents were so certain of their own beliefs that they could not open themselves to the new thing God was doing in Jesus Christ. " 'This people honors me with their lips, but their hearts are far from me; in vain do they worship me, teaching human precepts as doctrines.' You abandon the commandment of God and hold to human tradition" (Mark 7:6-8).

In a place of certitude, nothing can call into question our certainties and beliefs. Nothing puzzles us. Nothing requires exploration or revision. We are confident in our own righteousness. This version of works righteousness leaves no room for God's grace to break into our lives.

Critical thinking moves us beyond our certitudes and self-assurance to a place of exploration. Critical thinking helps us create the free, open, hospitable space within us and between us where we can explore what the Spirit says to the church.

Critical thinkers take their own thinking apart and examine it. They think not just about *what* they are thinking but also about *how* they are thinking it. Critical thinkers raise important questions and perspectives. They test their assumptions and beliefs. Critical thinkers possess genuine humility. They are conscious of the limits of their own knowledge. They are aware of how human sin results in self-deception and arrogance. They do not confuse their human knowledge with divine revelation.

Christian educators foster critical and creative reflection-in-action by equipping church members with tools for thinking about how they are thinking.

Dimensions of Critical Thinking

Critical thinking involves several basic dimensions of thought. These dimensions include purpose, viewpoint, information, concepts, conclusions, assumptions, and consequences.[1]

Purpose. All thinking is directed toward some goal or purpose we hope to achieve. Sometimes we are clear about the purpose toward which our thinking is directed. At other times, we have only a vague idea of our goals. In some cases, we hold contradictory purposes. We may want the church to grow but also want everything to stay exactly the same. We may want more children in Sunday school yet not want noise and confusion.

Effective thinkers take time to understand and state clearly the purposes they hope to achieve. They also dig beneath the surface to uncover why these purposes or outcomes are valuable or important to them. Effective thinkers work hard to choose purposes that are worthy of Christian faith. They seek to perceive where they may be embracing contradictory goals.

The governing board at First Church is clear about the congregation's purposes and goals. At the beginning of each meeting, members review the "Great Ends of the Church" from their denomination's book of order. Someone leads a brief Bible study on one end or purpose of the church each month. Members ask themselves how the church is doing in relation to this goal or purpose.

Church educators and leaders can pose several questions that help church boards and small groups foster clearer thinking about purposes or goals.

- What makes this activity or goal important to us?
- What will accomplishing this goal do for us?
- What will happen if we do not achieve this goal?
- Can we state our purpose or desired outcome in several different ways so that we are clearer about what we mean by it?
- What other purposes or goals do we have that might contradict this one?
- How significant is this purpose in the long run? Is it really what God would have us focus on?

Viewpoint. Situations are always seen from multiple viewpoints. People close to a situation will view it differently from those who are farther away. Some people focus on the big picture. They see the forest but may pay little attention to the individual trees. Others look at the trees and never see the forest.

Leaders at New York Avenue Church were trying to analyze the conflict between Mike and Fernando that had grown progressively worse during the last few months. Mike chaired the education committee. Fernando was chair of the trustees. At last week's church-council meeting, their frustration with one another boiled over into an angry outburst that soured the whole meeting.

"I think that when you solve a problem, you always have to address it at the level above where it is," Pastor Lon said. "So if Mike and Fernando are having problems working together, we need to address it at the level above them. That means having them get together and talk about the church's mission and vision. If we can get them to agree on the church's mission, then their conflict should disappear." Pastor Lon's viewpoint involved keeping his eyes on the big picture. If you focus on the big picture, then eventually all the little pieces fall into place.

Alexsandra, on the other hand, had a different viewpoint. "Well, it's just a personality conflict between Mike and Fernando," she replied. "They are so different that they will never get along. We need to elect other people to chair the trustees and the education committee."

"Well, I disagree with both of you," Burt added. "I think the problem is organizational. The education committee sees the children in our neighborhood and the impact they are having on our Sunday school and Wednesday night programs. But the trustees are not in the building on Wednesday. On Sunday they go to the sanctuary and never come near the education wing. So they don't see all these new kids. All they see are dollars and insurance liability," he continued. "So you have two people whose behavior is being driven by how close their respective groups are to the actual situation."

Pastor Lon, Alexsandra, and Burt all had different viewpoints. One saw everything through the big picture of mission and vision. A second focused on individuals and their temperaments. Still another used the lens of organizational behavior. The viewpoint we adopt will determine the diagnosis we make. Our diagnosis, in turn, shapes what actions we prescribe.

Effective thinkers are clear about their viewpoint. They seek to understand viewpoints and perspectives other than their own, particularly when they hold passionate convictions about the correctness of their own point of view. They attempt to uncover their prejudices and biases. They can articulate their own viewpoint with its strengths and weaknesses. They can also state objectively points of view other than their own, even when they disagree with them. Critical thinkers explore how to frame and reframe a situation through the lens of different viewpoints.

Ineffective thinkers, if they think at all about viewpoints other than their own, immediately dismiss those viewpoints as irrelevant or incorrect. They are unable to state objectively someone else's point of view, particularly when it differs from their own. Ineffective thinkers usually rely on narrow or superficial viewpoints.

Questions that encourage church members to inquire into their points of view are:
- Are we clear about our own point of view in this situation?
- Have we inquired into the viewpoints of others?
- Can we state clearly and objectively viewpoints other than our own?
- Where do we have difficulty appreciating others' viewpoints? What prevents us from entering into them more fully?
- How could where we are standing in relation to this situation be influencing our point of view?
- What other scenarios could plausibly describe this problem or situation from another viewpoint?
- What would we see if we reframed this situation from several other viewpoints?

Information. Our thinking is only as sound as the information on which it is based. We often fail to realize how much the quality of information influences our thinking and acting.

Ineffective thinkers display overconfidence in their own information. They are sure they have enough information and it is the right information. The result is a confirmation bias in which they favor data that supports their current assumptions while they discount information that challenges their assumptions.

Ineffective thinkers tend to rely on information that is easily available. But the most readily available data may not be the most relevant or the most reliable data. It takes time and energy to get the facts needed to make a good decision. But church members are usually volunteers operating under time constraints. As a result, they often gather the information that can be acquired with the least trouble or effort, even when it is not the best or most relevant information.

A third problem for ineffective thinkers is their tendency to be biased by a recency effect. They draw parallels between the current situation and a recent, similar experience. Rather than delve into the deeper dynamics and realities of a situation, they presume it is just like another recent experience.

Ineffective thinkers also suffer from a vividness bias. Vivid information is more easily recalled. Thus, people are more likely to use vivid data in decision making and problem solving even when it lacks real relevance.

Effective thinkers, on the other hand, understand how overconfidence in their own judgment can cause them to fail to collect and genuinely consider key information. They attempt to collect accurate, relevant data. They test whether they are drawing conclusions that can be supported by the actual data.

"We face a financial crisis going into the last quarter of the year," Mitch announced to the church council. "Our income is behind monthly projections. If we don't start cutting staff and programs, we will be awash in red ink by December."

"Mitch is right," added Ginger, "I certainly don't want to face again the kind of crisis we had at the end of last year." Around the table, heads began to nod approvingly.

"Now wait a minute, Mitch," Carol objected. "As I look at this information you gave us, you've divided the budget by 12 and projected how much we should receive each month to stay on target. But is that really how people pay their pledges? I know we miss some summer months when we are up at the lake. And then we catch up in December. I'm wondering if you have an actual month-by-month cash flow analysis to show us."

"No, I don't." Mitch responded crankily. "But I do have these numbers. And they show we've got a problem."

"Well," Carol answered, "Those are the most readily available numbers. But I'm not sure they are the best data for making this kind of decision. They may not be giving us a true picture of our situation."

"I agree with Carol," Tim added. "When you said something about last year's finances, I could feel my stomach tighten up. That experience is so recent and so vivid that I find it hard to think beyond it. At the same time, I'm not sure we'll be making the best decision if we just use what you've brought tonight."

Tim and Carol illustrate effective critical thinkers. They are much more careful in how they use information to think about decisions and problems. They are aware how information can influence their conclusions and are more careful with data.

Effective critical thinkers ask questions like:
- Where can we look for information that disproves or contradicts what our data suggest?

- Have we honestly considered information that might conflict with our position?
- Does our claim go further than what the evidence can support?
- Are we distorting information to make our position stronger?
- How accurate and relevant is our information?
- How has the vividness, recency, or availability of information influenced our thinking?

Concepts. We cannot talk about anything without using concepts. They are like the air we breathe. Some concepts come from theories or philosophies that shape how we see the world. An accountant, for example, will use a variety of theories and concepts to interpret her congregation's financial reports. The mission chairperson, who is not an accountant, may look at these same reports through a quite different set of concepts that are shaped by his theological commitments.

In addition to explicit conceptual frameworks, we also rely on implicit, taken-for-granted concepts and theories. We all use rules of thumb to make our thinking easier. A carpenter may apply his "measure twice and cut once" rule of thumb to more than just a construction project.

Effective thinkers are aware of what concepts they are using and how these concepts color their thinking. Ineffective thinkers are unaware of how concepts and theories influence their thinking. They often are unclear about the basic meaning of terms or words they use. They are not careful how they phrase their ideas and may use an expression or word that confuses or negatively impacts hearers.

We can improve our critical thinking by asking certain questions about the concepts or theories that inform our thinking:

- What kinds of concepts or theories are we using to understand this situation?
- What are the strengths and weaknesses of these concepts or theories?
- What other concepts or theories could we use to help us think about this situation?
- What do we know that we do not know?
- What concepts or key terms are others using as they talk about this situation? What is the impact of these terms or concepts?

Conclusions and Assumptions. Conclusions and assumptions always mutually influence one another. One flaw in our thinking is to confuse an assumption with a conclusion.

A conclusion is a determination that something is true based on something else being correct or true. A conclusion can therefore be accurate or inaccurate depending upon the information that an individual is using. I see dark clouds and hear thunder. I therefore conclude that I had better close my car windows because a rainstorm is coming.

An assumption, on the other hand, is something taken for granted or assumed. We do not question our assumptions. They are not based on evidence or facts. Assumptions usually develop from something we previously experienced or learned but now no longer question. Assumptions become self-evident but unconscious rules about reality that we use to reach conclusions.

Our conclusions are usually closely related to our assumptions. In fact, we typically base our conclusions on taken-for-granted assumptions rather than on information. We draw conclusions so quickly that we are unaware of the assumptions undergirding them. Differing assumptions account for why two people can reach different conclusions about the same situation.

Because they are so closely related, people often confuse information, assumptions, and conclusions. We draw a conclusion and then treat our conclusion as if it were factual information rather than an inference we have reached.

I am driving on a rural road in my county. I look into my rearview mirror and see a sheriff's patrol car. It follows me for about five minutes. I conclude that I must have done something wrong and will soon be pulled over and ticketed. In this situation, I took information (a patrol car was following me) and reached a conclusion (I will be pulled over and ticketed) based on an assumption (patrol cars do not follow someone for several miles unless they are waiting to pull them over) [see Figure 7.1].

Figure 7.1: Conclusions and Assumptions

Information	Conclusion	Assumption
A sheriff's patrol car is following me.	I am going to get a ticket.	Patrol cars only follow you if you have done something wrong.

Joe teaches the sixth-grade Sunday school class at Faith Church. Sammie has missed class for the past three Sundays. Joe concludes that Sammie is upset over something that happened and is intentionally staying away. But Sammie is really absent because he was sick for one Sunday and his family was on vacation the other two weeks. Joe used some concrete data (Sammie's three-week absence) to reach a totally incorrect conclusion (Sammie is upset about something that happened in class) based on an unexamined assumption he holds (if people are absent from a Sunday school class more than two weeks in a row it is because they are angry).

Assumptions and conclusions are so interwoven with our thought processes that we cannot become critical thinkers without continually surfacing and examining these two components of thinking. Critical thinkers are clear about the conclusions they are reaching and the assumptions that underlie these conclusions. They reach conclusions that follow reasonably from the information or evidence they have. Critical thinkers also strive to understand the unspoken assumptions behind their conclusions. They analyze where these assumptions originally came from and how well these assumptions currently serve them in creating the life they want.

Uncritical thinkers are unaware of their assumptions. They make assumptions about situations that are unreasonable or unjustified. They are unaware of the unconscious and sometimes destructive rules that guide their actions. Rather than trying to understand and update their assumptions, they ignore them.

Questions that encourage critical thinking about assumptions and conclusions are:
- How will we know if we have solved this problem effectively?
- How will we know if we have identified the core issue?
- Do our conclusions follow from the information?
- What filter of assumptions are we using to look at this information?
- What assumed facts are we taking for granted?
- What assumptions are other people making?
- If we had other assumptions, what conclusions could we reach from this same information?
- What conclusions would someone totally different from us reach using this same information?

Consequences or Implications. People often fail to think through the implications and consequences of a desired course of action. Every action can have three kinds of implications: possible ones, probable ones, and necessary ones. Every time I get in my car and drive down the highway it is possible that I could be in an accident. It is probable that I will be in an accident if I am talking on the cell phone, browsing through a magazine, or shaving while I drive. Implications are thus what may happen in a situation. Consequences, on the other hand, are what actually occur.

Many times people do not think through all the implications of their actions. Their decisions thus have unintended consequences. The trustees at Hope Church wanted to pave the parking lot. People were tracking dirt and gravel into the building on Sundays. Gravel and dirt made more work for the custodian and created wear-and-tear on the floors. The trustees concluded that if they paved the parking lot, it would actually save money since building maintenance would be reduced.

So the trustees aggressively raised funds for a $120,000 paving project. The finance committee objected to this campaign, saying it was too close to the church's annual stewardship drive and would bleed resources away from the regular budget. In fact, the trustees did meet their goal, and giving to the operational and mission budgets was down. The trustees had not thought this was a possible or even probable implication of their project. Yet it became a real consequence for the church's annual budget.

Critical thinkers examine implications. They consider the negative as well as the positive potential results of their choices. Uncritical thinkers seldom imagine multiple implications. They overfocus on the positive consequences they desire and fail to take into account the possibility of negative or unexpected consequences.

We can increase our ability to think critically about consequences and implications by asking questions like:
- Have we thought through all the significant consequences that could occur as a result of this action?

- If we make this decision, what other consequences could follow that we have not considered?
- Have we overfocused on the positive consequences of our actions or decisions? What possible negative consequences might occur?
- What events beyond our control might affect this decision's consequences?

Each Dimension Influences the Others

These dimensions of critical thinking influence one another. The quality of one dimension affects the quality of the others. A change in one dimension ripples through the others. Our viewpoint, for example, shapes what information we see as significant. Our assumptions often determine our purposes, which influence the conclusions we reach.

The interweaving of these dimensions means that questions we ask ourselves about any one dimension will inevitably trigger questions about how we are construing another dimension. Powerful questions are not limited to dialogue in a Sunday school classroom or midweek Bible study. Posing powerful questions to a church board or committee can encourage new insights and learning that extend far beyond the immediate issue under discussion. Powerful learning cannot be contained. It cascades through our thinking, feeling, and acting.

STANDARDS OF CRITICAL THINKING

Critical thinkers also have explicit standards to judge the adequacy of their thinking. These standards include clarity, accuracy, precision, relevance, fairness, and breadth.[2]

Clarity. Clarity is the foundation upon which the remaining standards are built. If a thought is unclear, no one knows about its accuracy, depth, relevance, or significance.

Even when we believe we are being clear about our thoughts, we often are not. "Frieda is a good church worker," Rosa says to other members of the committee on lay leadership. "She would be great serving on the church council." Others around the table nod their heads and soon Frieda's name is slotted for an at-large church-council position. But what does Rosa really mean by "good church worker"? Rosa's statement is so vague that everyone around the table can give her words their own interpretation, all of which might be different from Rosa's. Rosa's statement would have been clearer if she had said: "Frieda is well organized. She is able to say what she thinks without becoming hostile or accusatory. And she listens well. I think these are gifts needed on a policy-making body like the church council."

Questions that raise our awareness about clarity include:
- What is an example of what we are saying?
- Can we illustrate what we mean when we say this?
- How could we elaborate on what we mean?

Accuracy. A statement can be clear but still not be accurate. If I say, "I have a million dollars in the bank," I am being clear but totally inaccurate. People sometimes misrepresent facts unintentionally to put themselves in the best light possible. People sometimes make inaccurate statements to bolster their own position or undermine someone else's argument. We sometimes believe that our thoughts are accurate simply because they are our thoughts. Conversely, we all have an inclination to doubt the accuracy of information that contradicts what we believe or desire while accepting at face value information supporting our own viewpoint.

Critical thinkers assess the accuracy of their own perspectives as well as those with which they disagree. They seek to verify the accuracy of statements. They are careful to state accurately their own assertions and perceptions. They ask questions like:

- How can we check to see if our information is accurate?
- How could our commitment to a particular viewpoint be causing us to misrepresent information?
- Where would we look for information that contradicts our position?

Precision. A statement can be clear and accurate but not precise. I ask my son Jonathan if there is milk in the refrigerator before I pour my cereal into a bowl. "Yes," he answers, "There is milk in the refrigerator." When I get the milk container, however, it only has a few drops of milk in it. Jonathan's statement is clear and accurate. But it is not precise. We are precise when we give enough information for someone to understand clearly the actual situation.

"Attendance is down in our youth fellowship," Art said. "I am concerned that we may not have the right people working with our youth." From across the table, Odette asked, "How much is it down? Before I know whether there's a problem, I need to have more precise numbers."

Art's statement was clear and accurate. But it lacked precision. His imprecise numbers could have left the education ministry area with a false impression of serious decline.

Critical thinkers ask:

- Can we be more specific?
- Can we have or give more details?

Relevance. Statements can be clear, accurate, and precise but absolutely irrelevant to the topic under consideration. Our usual reaction to someone else's irrelevant statement is "What's that got to do with anything?" But we are much less quick to observe our own irrelevant thinking.

Critical thinkers carefully monitor how relevant a particular thought, observation, or fact is to a topic.

- What connection does this have to the topic we are discussing?
- How does this perception relate to that idea?

Fairness. Human beings are prone to self-deception. To be concerned about our tendency to distort and to manipulate is to take the doctrine of sin seriously. When we think from a self-centered perspective we often succeed in deceiving ourselves. As a result, we distort our opponents' positions or bend information to our own purposes rather than treat it with integrity.

Critical thinkers examine whether they are being fair-minded in their thinking.

- Are we distorting someone else's perspective to make our own sound more appealing?
- Are we using a reasonable, logical argument backed by objective facts to obtain some self-serving goal?
- Are we twisting the meaning of words or manipulating numbers or facts to prove a point in order to secure our own interests?

The standard of fairness asks whether we are seeking truth and truthfulness or merely trying to get what we want.

Breadth. Narrow-minded thinkers lack breadth. They do not try to understand alternative viewpoints. They refuse to explore perspectives opposed to their own. Thinking can be clear, accurate, precise, and relevant but utterly lacking in breadth. One of the primary ways we avoid losing our desired objective is to refuse even to entertain alternative points of view. We unconsciously tell ourselves that if we actually considered another viewpoint, we might find ourselves reconsidering our own views.

Critical thinkers, on the other hand, are willing to entertain alternative perspectives. They know that they can become stuck in a perspective that limits their vision. Being stuck in one, narrow-minded perspective means that we limit the resources and possibilities available to us. Critical thinkers ask themselves:

- From what other perspectives could we consider this topic?
- How many different ways could we look at this issue?
- If we looked at this from the perspective of someone totally opposite from ourselves, what would we see?

Abbey and Meg had been given the task of redesigning the Sunday school program. They knew that some people were convinced the only option was to move to the rotation model. Other members of the Education Ministry Team were equally committed to a traditionally graded Sunday school. Still others favored an intergenerational educational program that combined adults, youth, and children in a variety of nontraditional learning activities.

At the ministry team meeting, Abbey and Meg outlined a large, spoked wheel on the carpet with masking tape. In some wedges, they placed a card describing that wedge [see Figure 7.2].

Abbey explained that each wedge represented a perspective on what should be done with the Sunday school. The "Everything's OK" perspective meant things were really going fine and nothing should be changed. The "Getting Together" perspective was for those who advocated an intergenerational model. The "Let's Rotate" perspective represented those who favored a rotation model. Another possible perspective, Abbey said, was the "Time Change" perspective. It was for people who thought the problem was the Sunday morning schedule for worship and Sunday school. "Move to Midweek" was for those who wanted to abandon Sunday morning education and move everything to the Wednesday afterschool hour. The "Full Steam Ahead" perspective was for those who wanted to keep things the same but try harder.

Figure 7.2: Meg and Abbey's Perspective Wheel on Sunday School Options

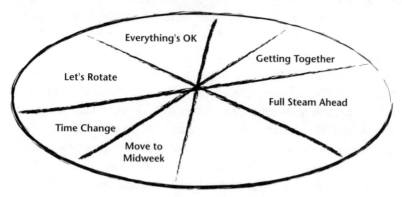

Meg next asked the team members to name the two remaining wedges. Members brainstormed possibilities and finally agreed on the "New Space" perspective—what the Sunday school really needed was renovated space—and the "Zip Drive" perspective—introducing computers and other high-tech resources would revitalize the Sunday school. Meg wrote these words on cards and placed them in the final two wedges.

Abbey then asked everyone to go to the wedge that best represented his or her own perspective. She next invited people in each wedge to describe how Sunday school felt in that perspective. They also shared what they thought the benefits or advantages of that perspective were and the costs or disadvantages.

When everyone had finished, Abbey asked group members to move to the wedge that they thought their children or grandchildren would be in. "Don't rush to any one wedge," Abbey said. "Try to stand in several wedges and test out how they feel before settling on the one you want to be in." Once again, Abbey asked members to share what that perspective felt like as well as its costs and benefits.

"Now move again," said Meg. "This time go to the perspective you think your best friend would want you to be in." Once participants had settled on a perspective, Meg announced, "Take some time in silence just to be in this perspective. Really let yourself feel what it's like to be here. Then we'll talk about what we notice about this perspective."

After some discussion, Meg moved participants again. "Go this time to the perspective you least want to be in. And then allow yourself to be open to what it would be like. What would you see here? What could you create from here? What would you give up being here?" After a few minutes, everyone again talked about feelings and thoughts. They then asked participants to move back to the table, sit down, and make a few notes on what they had experienced.

After this experience, team members had a different conversation about the Sunday school than they otherwise would have had. Meg and Abbey helped members step outside their own perspectives and see the situation from other points of view. The exercise loosened the grip of a particular perspective or viewpoint and allowed members to take a broader view.

CRITICAL THINKING AND CHRISTIAN FAITH FORMATION

Christian communities need to think about more than how they are thinking. They also need to read, learn, mark, and inwardly digest Christian Scripture and tradition. Critical thinking plays a crucial role in any form of reflection-in-action, including theological reflection. But critical thinking is only a tool for theological reflection, not a substitute for it.

God comes to us through our experiences. We believe that God's Word becomes flesh in Jesus' life, death, and resurrection. God reveals God's self in human experience and human form. As a result, all human experience has the capacity to reveal who God is and what God does. God comes to us and communicates with us through a medium we can understand: human experience itself. Reflection on our human experience becomes the doorway through which we discover how to love, know, and serve God more fully.

Christians also believe in the doctrine of revelation. God's mighty acts in human history reveal God's power, purpose, and presence. God speaks in the garden in the cool of the evening. God speaks from a burning bush. God calls Isaiah as he stands worshiping in the Temple. God comes to us through bread and wine. There is no separate category of life called "religious experience" that reveals God to us. There is only the religious or spiritual dimension of all human experience. There is no experience of God that is not at the same time a human experience of something else. Human experience itself is radically sacramental. Life's basic experiences have the capacity to reveal God to us if we attend thoughtfully and prayerfully to them.

These experiences can distort and confuse as well as reveal. Sometimes we learn the wrong thing from experience. Sometimes we learn nothing from an experience. The Greek word for revelation literally means "to uncover." Critical reflection-in-action under the guidance of God's Spirit helps us uncover our hidden assumptions and taken-for-granted mental maps that limit or distort our awareness of God's call and claim upon our lives.

The raw word of daily experience requires interpretation if we are to discern God's providence and revelation within it. We bring this raw experience into conversation with the inherited experience of the community (Scripture and tradition) as well as the present experience of others within the Christian community.

Thoughtful, prayerful reflection on experience lies at the heart of transformative learning and Christian faith formation. Such reflection does not come automatically, however. It requires discipline and dialogue with others. It involves critical, creative, and prayerful thinking about our experiences.

Five Stages of Theological Reflection on Experience. Theological reflection involves five basic steps: reflecting on our lived experience, reflecting on Scripture and tradition, bringing Scripture and tradition into dialogue with our experience, listening for new meanings and truths, and planning for action [see Figure 7.3].

First, we identify a lived experience upon which we wish to reflect. Critical thinking plays a crucial role in helping us name and analyze our lived experience. The dimensions and standards of critical thinking allow us to probe beneath the surface of our experience

Figure 7.3: Basic Steps of Theological Reflection

Reflect on scripture and tradition

Reflect on lived experience

Bring experience and scripture/tradition into dialogue

Plan for new action

Listen for new meaning, truth

and understand how this experience is a window into our taken-for-granted assumptions and mental maps.

Second, we identify a biblical theme or text that we wish to bring into conversation with our experience and explore its meaning. We may intentionally seek a passage that correlates in some way with our experience. Or we may simply turn to the church's lectionary, confident that God's Spirit will speak to us through whatever Scripture passage we choose.

The same dimensions and standards of critical thinking we used to explore our own experience are also a rich resource for discovering the unsuspected depths of Christian Scripture and tradition. The same questions we pose of our own experience, we can ask of Scripture and tradition.

- What is its purpose?
- What are its implications? Its consequences?
- Does it have a viewpoint?
- What assumptions do we bring to it?
- What assumptions did its authors make?
- What assumptions are we making as we approach this passage?
- Did its authors have particular concepts that were guiding the writing and collection of this text? What were they?
- What concepts are we using to understand this passage?
- What are some alternative concepts that would result in a different understanding?
- Where am I stuck in a particular perspective about this text?
- What other perspectives exist and what is available or not available to me if I look at this text through those alternative perspectives?

Third, we bring the fruit of these two explorations into conversation with one another. All the guidelines and questions for authentic dialogue come to bear as we prompt this conversation.

Our fourth step is to identify new meanings or truths we can take from this dialogue between our experience and Christian wisdom.

- What have we learned?
- What new insights have come to us?
- How has the Spirit spoken to us?
- How have we been changed?

Here again the dimensions and standards of critical thinking can guide our reflection.

Finally, we ask what concrete actions we will take as a result of our reflection. Reflection is for the sake of action in our lives.

- How has this theological reflection deepened our learning?
- How has it forwarded the action in our lives?
- What is God calling us to be or to do as a result of our reflection?

The tools of critical and creative thinking are not a separate stage in our reflection-in-action. They are interwoven into all aspects of theological reflection. These tools and strategies are useful not only in informal learning contexts but in formal settings as well [see Figure 7.4].

CONCLUSION

Christian community cannot exist except as a learning community, because discipleship and learning go together. "Take my instruction instead of silver, and knowledge rather than choice gold; for wisdom is better than jewels, and all that you may desire cannot compare with her" (Proverbs 8:10-11). The appropriate stance before God is an available heart and a teachable spirit. "Teach me your way, O LORD, that I may walk in your truth; give me an undivided heart to revere your name" (Psalm 86:11).

Learning is a profoundly spiritual experience fraught with possibilities for both good and evil. Paradoxically, the Bible suggests that to learn separates us from God and also leads us to God. Adam and Eve eat the fruit of the tree giving them knowledge of good and evil. They learn a knowledge that alienates humanity from God and itself. God then expels humankind from paradise. But paradise is not destroyed, only guarded by cherubim (Genesis 3:24).

The Book of Exodus later narrates the story of God's drawing one people, Israel, back into a special relationship. On Mt. Sinai, God gives Moses the covenant teachings that bind Israel to God. God then tells Moses to place these teachings in the ark of the covenant. Hovering over the ark are two cherubim, like those who stand at the gates of paradise. The symbolism is too obvious to deny: Learning God's covenant wisdom is the gateway back to paradise. "Know that the LORD is God. ... Enter [these] gates with thanksgiving, and [these] courts with praise" (Psalm 100:3-4). One kind of learning separates us from God. Another unites us with God.

The gospels describe Jesus' followers as disciples; the Greek word that is used literally means "learners." Jesus' most common title in the gospels is "teacher" or "Rabbi." The

Figure 7.4: Critical Thinking and Theological Reflection

Step in Theological Reflection	Dimensions of Critical Thinking	Standards of Critical Thinking

Analyzing Lived Experience	What was my purpose in this experience?
	
	From what viewpoint am I looking at this experience?
	
	What information is important in describing this experience? Why?
	
	What concepts am I using to analyze this experience?
	
	How have I reached conclusions about this experience?
	
	What am I taking for granted? Assuming?
	
	What are the implications and consequences of this experience?
		Am I describing this experience
		  Clearly?
		  Accurately?
		  Precisely?
		  Fairly?
		  Broadly?
		Is this a relevant experience to bring to this reflection?

Exploring Scripture and Tradition	What is the purpose of this text?
	
	What is the viewpoint of the author of this text?
	
	What information does the author treat as important?
	
	What concepts were the authors of this text using to guide their thinking and writing?
	
	What concepts am I using to approach this text? What other concepts could I use that would result in a different outcome?
	
	What do the authors of this text assume? What am I assuming as I approach this passage?
	
	What are the implications and consequences of this text?
		Is this a relevant text?
		Is my reading of this text
		  Clear?
		  Accurate?
		  Precise?
		  Fair?
		  Broad enough to take into consideration other interpretations?

Facilitating a Dialogue Between Experience and Text	What is the purpose of this dialogue? Are we staying focused on our main purpose?
	
	Are we listening for others' viewpoints and able to summarize them accurately?
	
	Are we being clear about words, terms, or concepts we are using in our dialogue?
		Are we speaking and listening
		  Clearly?
		  Accurately?
		  Precisely?
		  Fairly?
		  Broadly?

	How might something we are all assuming or taking for granted become a barrier to dialogue?	
	How will we know when our dialogue has reached its conclusion?	
	Are we prepared for consequences of dialogue, such as changing our own perspectives or opinions?	

Gleaning New Meaning and Truth	Have I gained a clear purpose?	Are new meanings or truths
		  Clear?
		  Accurate in representing this reflection?
		  Precisely stated?
		  Relevant to my life?
		  Fair to the text and my experience?
		  Broad enough?

	Can this reflection alter my viewpoint on a situation or person?	
	What information about my experience or this text is important to me now?	
	What concepts can I take from this reflection that will inform my being and acting?	
	What conclusions have I reached about myself? The world? God?	
	What have I learned about my taken-for-granted assumptions?	
	What are the implications and consequences of new meanings or truths I have gained?	

Planning for New Action	Is the purpose of my action clear?	Is my plan....
		  Clear?
		  Accurate?
		  Precise?
		  Relevant to the situation?
		  Fair to everyone?
		  Broad enough?

	From what viewpoint or viewpoints am I planning my actions?	
	What information do I need in order to make and implement my plans?	
	What concepts am I using to plan my action?	
	What conclusions have I reached about what I shall do?	
	What may I be assuming?	
	What are the potential implications and consequences of my plans?	

modern church seldom uses this title because it does not reflect our Christological confessions. It does, however, communicate the centrality of teaching and learning in Jesus' own self-understanding and in the early church. Teaching and learning are central to discipleship because they lie at the heart of all transformation and maturation. We can physically grow simply by consuming food and drink. All other growth—whether emotional, psychological, or spiritual—occurs only through learning. "One does not live by bread alone, but by every word that comes from the mouth of God" (Matthew 4:4).

Conversion itself involves learning. It is a change in knowing, a transformation of the mental maps we use to navigate ourselves through life. Jesus comes announcing, "Repent, and believe in the good news" (Mark 1:15). Repentance has less to do with feeling sorry for what we have done than with learning to see ourselves and our world in a new way. To repent is to have a change of mind. Remember: The Greek word for repentance, *metanoia,* literally means a change of mind. Or, as Paul says to the church at Rome, "Do not be conformed to this world, but be transformed by the renewing of your minds, so that you may discern what is the will of God—what is good and acceptable and perfect" (Romans 12:2).

Despite learning's centrality, we have historically understood little about how the mind grows and learns. Aristotle, in the fourth century before Christ, watched headless chickens and decided that the heart rather than the brain is the seat of consciousness. In the seventeenth century, Rene Descartes described the pineal body (a small structure in the brain at the roof of the third ventricle) as the seat of the soul that motivates and guides our thinking.

About one hundred years ago, science began to study more rigorously the human brain. An Italian physician, Camillo Golgi, discovered in the 1870's how to make nerve cells visible under a microscope. By 1901 scientists had learned that neurons are separated by tiny gaps called synapses. In the 1950's Paul MacLean identified the limbic system and other scientists discovered that neurons are arranged in columns within the brain. During the 1980's the quickening pace of discovery and research established neuroscience as a major field of study. New instruments and procedures were invented, allowing researchers to look inside the brain and see what happens when we learn. We now know a great deal about how the brain learns and changes.

These discoveries have practical implications. They can transform Christian teaching and learning. They give church educators new tools for fulfilling their ancient mandate to make disciples of Jesus Christ so that the love of God and neighbor may increase in our fragmented and broken world.

Deepening Your Learning

1. Analyze a situation in your life by using the dimensions and standards of critical thinking. What do you find difficult? What new insight about your situation do you experience?

2. Explore a situation in your life by using the perspective wheel described in the section on standards of critical thinking. Be sure to generate at least eight different perspectives. Identify the advantages and disadvantages of each one. How does this exercise change your thinking about the situation? Where might you use this exercise as a Christian educator?

3. Use the five-step model of theological reflection to explore a lived experience in your own life. What works for you? What does not work? How can you change the process so it serves you better? How can you use this revised model in your teaching and faith formation?

4. If you have been meeting as a group, what is next for you? Will you continue to meet to support your continuing growth and learning as Christian educators? Is there another book or resource you might study? If you are disbanding, what do you need to say or do at your final session so everyone feels complete and has closure?

ENDNOTES

1 Information about these dimensions is based in part on *Critical Thinking: Tools for Taking Charge of Your Professional and Personal Life,* by Richard W. Paul and Linda Elder (Financial Times/Prentice Hall, 2002).

2 Much of the material on standards of critical thinking is drawn from *Critical Thinking: Tools for Taking Charge of Your Professional and Personal Life,* by Richard W. Paul and Linda Elder (Financial Times/Prentice Hall, 2002).

Glossary

Accommodation. Piaget's term for the creation or major restructuring of mental maps or schemas. Our thinking accommodates itself to experienced reality.

Advance Organizer. A preliminary statement or reading that helps learners connect new knowledge to what they already know by reminding them of similarities between their prior knowledge and new information.

Amygdala. A structure within the limbic system that processes and stores strong emotional memories. It searches incoming sensory data for strong emotional threats and can activate a fight-flight response based on fuzzy, incomplete signals.

Assimilation. Piaget's term for the process by which more information or data is added to an existing mental map or schema. We assimilate additional knowledge into existing mental structures.

Axon. The extension on a neural cell that sends information to the dendrite of another neural cell.

Brainstem. Along with the cerebellum, constitutes the most primitive part of the brain, which we share with reptiles and other lower animals (*see* R-Brain). It controls many of our automatic functions, such as breathing and blood circulation.

Bridging Strategies. A family of learning strategies that help people make connections between new information and what they already know. Two basic bridging strategies are advance organizers and metaphors.

Cerebellum. Along with the brainstem, constitutes the most primitive part of the brain, which we share with reptiles and other lower animals (*see* R-Brain). It maintains the body's balance and muscle coordination.

Cerebrum. *See* Cortex.

Chunking Strategies. A family of learning strategies that break down large amounts of information into smaller "chunks" that are more easily learned and recalled.

Concrete Operational Stage. The third of Piaget's developmental stages (ages 7-11) during which children exhibit extremely concrete, literal thinking.

Conjunctive Faith. A stage of faith development (approximately midlife) in Fowler's faith development model. During this stage, adults reintegrate the values and beliefs they left behind in earlier stages. They develop a tolerance for ambiguity and paradox.

Cortex. The cortex consists of the cerebrum and neocortex and contains what is uniquely human in the brain. Thinking and speech reside in the cortex.

Cortisol. A chemical produced in the adrenal glands located above the kidneys. It is a stress-related substance that is released as part of our fight-flight response and can be toxic to the brain. It interrupts transmission of messages from neuron to neuron.

Dendrite. The extension on a neural cell that receives information from the axon of another neural cell.

Downshift. We have an R-brain "downshift" when our thinking becomes automatic, reactive, and concerned with survival under stressful or threatening conditions. When a downshift occurs, people have great difficulty thinking and learning.

Formal Operational Stage. The fourth of Piaget's developmental stages (ages 11 and up) during which people can think hypothetically or metaphorically and acquire the capacity to take alternative perspectives.

Fowler, James. A researcher who described a seven-stage model of faith development widely used in religious education.

Frames, Framing. A family of learning strategies that use matrix—or chartlike—structures to help people learn and recall knowledge.

Glial Cells. Brain cells that assist neurons in their migration during early brain development. They feed and "do housekeeping" for neurons.

Hippocampus. A structure in the limbic system that plays a major role in the storing and recall of sensory information. It is to the brain what a card catalog is to a library.

Hypothalamus. A part of the brain that lies below the thalamus and functions to regulate some metabolic processes and autonomic activities.

Individuative-Reflective Faith. A stage of faith development (ages 18-40) in Fowler's seven-stage developmental model. During this stage young adults think critically about the faith they created in the previous stage and separate their personal beliefs from those of the groups to which they belong.

Intuitive-Projective Faith. A stage of faith development (ages 2-7) in Fowler's seven-stage developmental model. During this stage the child projects himself or herself into stories and narratives through the active use of imagination and fantasy.

Kohlberg, Lawrence. A researcher who described a six-stage model of moral development.

Limbic System. Our mammalian brain. It is composed of several small structures that communicate chemically with every cell in the body. It is responsible for our emotions such as playfulness, nurture, and emotional bonding.

Mapping Strategies. A family of learning strategies that help people recall information by visually mapping significant concepts and the relationships between them.

Mental Maps or Mental Models (also called schemas). The internal mental assumptions, beliefs, rules, or scripts we develop to help us make sense of our experience and our world.

Myelin. A fatty substance that coats the axon of a neuron and allows messages to travel more quickly between neural cells.

Mythic-Literal Faith. A stage of faith (ages 7-12) in Fowler's seven-stage developmental model. During this stage, the child focuses on facts and literal meanings.

Neocortex. *See* Cortex.

Neural Branching. A family of learning strategies that enrich neural networks and broaden interconnectivity within the brain.

Neural Hijacking. A term used to describe how the amygdala can activate a fight-flight response on the basis of fuzzy, incomplete data.

Neuron. A brain cell or neural cell.

Neurotransmitters. Chemical molecules that carry information from one neuron to another. More than fifty neurotransmitters are known to exist, including many peptides.

Peptides. A class of chemical compounds produced by the body. Peptides can function as neurotransmitters.

Piaget, Jean. A twentieth-century scientist who described how our thinking and perceiving develops and changes as we grow.

Preoperational Stage. The second of Piaget's developmental stages (ages 2-7) during which children acquire language and the ability to use symbols.

R-Brain. A term for the brainstem and cerebellum considered as a unit. The expression "R-brain" highlights the automatic, reactive response we have to threatening or stressful situations.

Resistance. The unconscious emotional process of slowing down or blocking the learning or change process. It occurs when people become fearful of losing something important to them.

Schema. *See* Mental Maps or Mental Models.

Schema Attack. A negative consequence of our mental maps. Schema attacks involve jumping to conclusions, selective perceptions, or knee-jerk responses to people or situations based on our assumptive frameworks or mental maps.

Sensorimotor Stage. The first of Piaget's developmental stages (birth to age 2) during which children know the world only through physical interaction.

Serotonin. An important neurotransmitter. Its presence allows messages to move swiftly between neurons. When serotonin levels drop, people may become depressed or have difficulty thinking clearly.

Synapse. The gap between the axon of one neuron and the dendrite of another. Information must leap across this gap to pass from one cell to another. Neurotransmitters play an essential role in moving messages across this gap or synapse.

Synthetic-Conventional Faith. A stage of faith (ages 12-18) in Fowler's seven-stage developmental model. During this stage, youth synthesize the community's stories into a personal story and internalize the community's norms and values.

Thalamus. A structure in the limbic system that acts as a relay or transfer station for sensory data arriving through the brainstem and being sent to the cerebral cortex.

Triune Brain. A term describing how the human brain consists of three unique parts: the R-brain, the limbic system, and the cortex.

Undifferentiated Faith. The first stage of faith development (birth to age 2) in Fowler's seven-stage developmental model.

Universalizing Faith. The final stage in Fowler's faith development model, a stage which is reached by only a few individuals. At this stage, individuals acquire a faith that looks beyond all boundaries and includes all people, cultures, and religions.

Bibliography

A Celebration of Neurons: An Educator's Guide to the Human Brain, by Robert Sylwester (Association for Supervision and Curriculum Development, 1995).

Critical Thinking: Tools for Taking Charge of Your Professional and Personal Life, by Richard W. Paul and Linda Elder (Financial Times/Prentice Hall, 2002).

Descartes' Error: Emotion, Reason, and the Human Brain, by Antonio R. Damasio (Quill/Harper-Collins, 1995).

The Dilemma of Enquiry and Learning, by Hugh G. Petrie (University of Chicago Press, 1981).

Emotional Alchemy: How the Mind Can Heal the Heart, by Tara Bennett-Goleman (Three Rivers Press, 2001).

Emotional Intelligence, by Daniel Goleman (Bantam Books, 1995).

A Failure of Nerve: Leadership in the Age of the Quick Fix, by Edwin H. Friedman (The Edwin Friedman Estate/Trust, 1999).

Frames of Mind: The Theory of Multiple Intelligences, by Howard Gardner (Basic Books, 1983).

Fundamentals of Cognitive Psychology, fifth edition, by Henry C. Ellis and R. Reed Hunt (WCB Brown & Benchmark, 1993).

Instructional Design: Implications From Cognitive Science, by Charles K. West, James A. Farmer, and Phillip M. Wolff (Prentice Hall, 1991).

Keeping in Touch: Christian Formation and Teaching, by Carol F. Krau (Discipleship Resources, 1999).

Learning and Instruction, by Richard Hamilton and Elizabeth Ghatala (McGraw-Hill, 1994).

Learning and Memory: Major Ideas, Principles, Issues, and Applications, by Robert W. Howard (Praeger, 1995).

Learning and Memory: The Brain in Action, by Marilee Sprenger (Association for Supervision and Curriculum Development, 1999).

Learning in Adulthood: A Comprehensive Guide, by Sharan B. Merriam and Rosemary S. Caffarella (Jossey-Bass, 1991).

Learning to Think, Learning to Learn: What the Science of Thinking and Learning Has to Offer Adult Education, by Jennifer Cromley, National Institute for Literacy Leader Fellowship Program Reports, Vol. 4, no. 1 (National Institute for Literacy, 2000).

Making Connections: Teaching and the Human Brain, by Renate Nummela Caine and Geoffrey Caine (Association for Supervision and Curriculum Development, 1991).

Our Spiritual Brain: Integrating Brain Research and Faith Development, by Barbara Bruce (Abingdon Press, 2002).

The Psychology of Moral Development: The Nature and Validity of Moral Stages, by Lawrence Kohlberg (Harper & Row, 1984).

The Quest for Mind: Piaget, Lévi-Strauss, and the Structuralist Movement, by Howard Gardner (Vintage Books, 1972).

"Seven Strategies That Encourage Critical Thinking," by Thomas Cardellichio and Wendy Field, in *Educational Leadership,* Vol. 54, no. 6, March 1997; pages 33-36.

Stages of Faith: The Psychology of Human Development and the Quest for Meaning, by James W. Fowler (Harper & Row, 1981).

Synaptic Self: How Our Brains Become Who We Are, by Joseph LeDoux (Viking, 2002).

Taxonomy of Educational Objectives: The Classification of Educational Goals, edited by Benjamin S. Bloom (David McKay Company, 1956).

Teaching With the Brain in Mind, by Eric Jensen (Association for Supervision and Curriculum Development, 1998).

The Three-Pound Universe, by Judith Hooper and Dick Teresi (Jeremy P. Tarcher, 1986).

"To Be Intelligent," by John Abbott, in *Educational Leadership,* Vol. 54, no. 6, March 1997; pages 6-10.

Why God Won't Go Away: Brain Science and the Biology of Belief, by Andrew Newberg, Eugene D'Aquili, and Vince Rause (Ballantine Books, 2001).